Tools of Timekeeping

A Kid's Guide *to the* History & Science *of* Telling Time

15

Hands-On Activities

Linda Formichelli & W. Eric Martin

nomad press

Nomad Press
A division of Nomad Communications
10 9 8 7 6 5 4 3 2 1
Copyright © 2005 by Nomad Press
ISBN: 0-9722026-7-6
Questions regarding the ordering of this book should be addressed to
Independent Publishers Group
814 N. Franklin St.
Chicago, IL 60610
www.ipgbook.com

Nomad Press
2456 Christian St.
White River Junction, VT 05001
www.nomadpress.net

Images courtesy of:
Pg. 7: Sun Calendar: http://www.bluehoney.org, Maya Calendar: http://www.astro.utu.fi;
Pg. 11: Gregorian Calendar: http://webexhibits.org/; **Pg. 16:** Egyptian Star Calendar: Moustafa
Gadalla www.egypt-tehuti.org/articles/egyptian-calendar.html; **Pg. 21:** Anaximander1:
http://www.ntsf.edu.cn; **Pg. 39:** Tower of the Winds – Catherine Yen; **Pg. 40:** Water Clock:
http://physics.nist.gov; **Pg. 44:** French Astrolabe Richard Paselk, Humboldt State University;
Pg. 52: Oil Clock: image courtesy of Collectiques.co.uk; **Pg. 61:** Su Sung's water clock:
http://physics.nist.gov; **Pg. 63:** Album 9 (Honnecourt Design): Ross Woodrow
http://www.newcastle.edu.au, Henlein's Nuremberg Egg: http://home.gci.net; **Pg. 72:** Galileo:
http://shl.stanford.edu/; **Pg. 73:** Galileo's Telescope: http://chemphys.phys.boun.edu.tr;
Pg. 76: Huygens: http://www.ady-bp.sulinet.hu; **Pg. 76:** Huygen's Pendulum clock: 1832
Edinburgh Encyclopaedia; **Pg. 79:** Harrison Escapement: Edinburgh Encyclopaedia; **Pg. 90-91:**
Time Zones: www.cia.gov/cia/publications/factbook/reference_maps/pdf/time_zones.pdf;
Pg. 95: Ben Franklin: http://www.soul.org; **Pg. 96:** Almanac: "Poor Richard, 1737, an almanac
for the Year of Christ 1737, by Richard Saunders, Philom." [Philadelphia: Franklin, 1736]; **Pg.
100** Franklin Pages: http://www.history.noaa.gov; **Pg. 101:** PierreMarie Curie: http://www.
cancoillotte.net; **Pg. 110:** First Atomic Clock: US Library of Congress Catalog Card Number: 65-
62472.; **Pg. 112:** http://tf.nist.gov; **Pg. 124:** Shuttle flame: http://shemesh.larc.nasa.gov; **Pg. 125:**
swirl: http://www.ing.iac.es; **Last page:** Chris Hardman www.ecocalendar.info.

Cover Images: Astrolabe, Waterclock: Richard Paselk, Humboldt State University

ACKNOWLEDGMENTS

Thanks to Lauri and Susan for reminding us that time waits for no one.
Without them, this book wouldn't have happened.

Contents

Introduction 1
Now Is the Time

Chapter One 3
The Birth of Time

Chapter Two 15
Here Come the Hours

Chapter Three 35
Telling Time After Twilight

Chapter Four 51
What Is a Clock Anyway?

Chapter Five 59
Escaping the Time Traps of Old

Chapter Six 69
Back and Forth and Back and Forth

Chapter Seven 83
Any Way You Slice It

Chapter Eight 99
Crystal Clear Timekeeping

Chapter Nine 109
Measuring Time Without Moving

Chapter Ten 117
Time On Your Hands

ACTIVITIES

Chapter One
Reading Seasons From a Shadow 11

Chapter Two
Tracking Hours Like an Egyptian 18
Finding Your Latitude 24
Build Your Own Sundial 25

Chapter Three
Watching the Hours Flow By 36
Make Your Own Sandglass 43
Finding Time in the Stars 46

Chapter Four
Burning the Midnight Wax 53
Make a Hand Sundial 57
Make Your Own Incense Clock 58

Chapter Six
Putting Pendulum Power to the Test 74
Looking for Longitude 81

Chapter Seven
What a Difference a Day Makes 84

Chapter Eight
Test Your Timing Reflex 108

Chapter Nine
Finding a Quarter in a Haystack 116

Chapter Ten
Dawn of a New Day 120

Now Is the Time

Time is a funny thing. We keep time, we save time, we lose time, we buy time, we make time when we're running late. People ask if we have the time, and we answer them as if we do. We talk about time as if it were an object that we can touch and feel, but of course time isn't like that at all.

Time is, as the joke goes, the universe's way of keeping everything from happening all at once. Try to imagine a world without time; you'd be ten years old, forty years old, forty-one years old, and not even born all at once. Trees in a forest would be saplings and towering giants simultaneously. Night and day, winter and summer—everything would happen at once, and you would get very, very confused. Your teacher might accuse you of not handing in your homework, while you swear that you did. Oddly, you would both be correct!

Even though we can't point to time or put time on a leash and take it for a walk, we can keep track of it by looking at the world around us: The earth spins, and the sun rises and falls. The seasons change, and your hair grows longer. Running water

1

erodes rock and creates canyons, and an egg in a pan cooks over heat.

Things change in the world, and we want to know how long it takes for them to change. When will the weather turn warm again? When will you arrive at school if you leave the house when the sun is on the horizon? How long do you have to wait before you can eat that egg?!?

Tools of Timekeeping explores how mankind has used the changing world to track time and explains how you can use tools and supplies found around the house to make clocks similar to those of your ancestors of long ago, and lots of other fun projects. Time can be a tricky topic, but by the end of this book, you should have a handle on time—if time could have a handle in the first place, that is.

THE BIRTH OF TIME

Imagine that on a school field trip your class becomes stranded in the woods, in a grassy field, or on an island in the Pacific Ocean. You have nothing with you except the clothes on your back and the sandwiches in your knapsacks. You have no cell phones, no watches, no complex tools of any kind. What do you do?

This situation might seem scary, but the first humans lived like this for thousands of years. Without hotels, drive-through windows, and refrigerators, they lived in caves and hunted their own food. Eventually they learned to build their own shelter and grow their own crops. As the seasons changed they followed herds of animals that migrated across the land. To prepare for

Track time by the sun and the moon

Explore different kinds of calendars

Learn how the months got their names

Read the seasons through shadows

3

winter, they made coats from animal pelts and smoked meat to eat while the animals hibernated.

Time at the beginning of human civilization was much simpler than it is today. Seconds, hours, weeks, months—none of them existed. The only units of time were those that people could track with the naked eye. A day was made up of dawn, noon, and dusk, which means our ancestors had no nine-to-five jobs or five o'clock shadow!

The night sky marked the passage of time, and humans learned to track the moon through its phases. As new moon followed new moon, the seasons changed, and as the seasons passed, the height of the noon sun rose and fell.

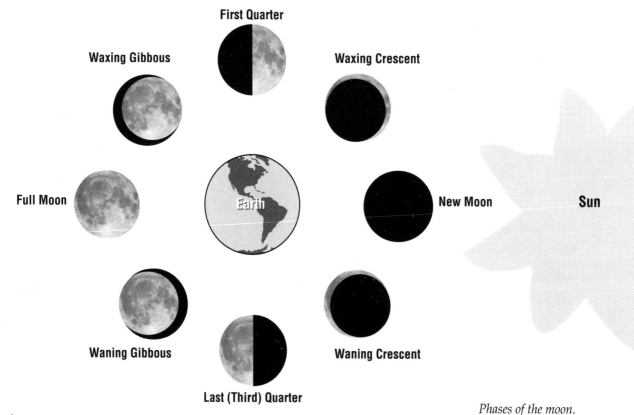

Phases of the moon.

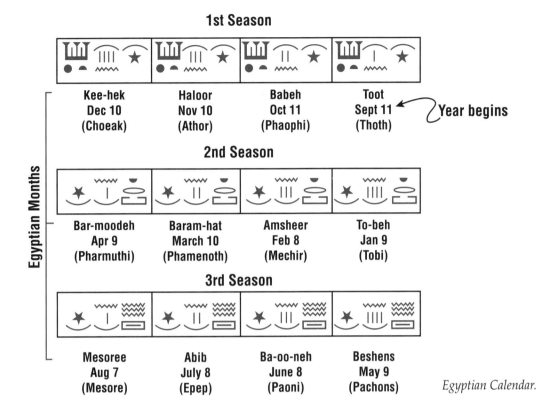

1st Season

Kee-hek Dec 10 (Choeak)	Haloor Nov 10 (Athor)	Babeh Oct 11 (Phaophi)	Toot Sept 11 (Thoth)

Year begins

2nd Season

Egyptian Months

Bar-moodeh Apr 9 (Pharmuthi)	Baram-hat March 10 (Phamenoth)	Amsheer Feb 8 (Mechir)	To-beh Jan 9 (Tobi)

3rd Season

Mesoree Aug 7 (Mesore)	Abib July 8 (Epep)	Ba-oo-neh June 8 (Paoni)	Beshens May 9 (Pachons)

Egyptian Calendar.

Humanity's first efforts at timekeeping consisted of tracking the movement of the sun, moon, planets, and stars. Over 20,000 years ago, European hunters scratched lines and made holes in bones and sticks. Experts think these marks were made to record the phases of the moon. With this simple beginning, mankind's first calendar was born.

The moon remained mankind's most important "clock" for thousands of years. The first Egyptian calendars, made before 4000 BCE, had three seasons (flood, seed time, and harvest) that each lasted four lunar months. (A lunar month, the time from one new moon to the next, lasts 29.5 days.) By 2000 BCE, the Babylonians had also developed a 12-month year, with months alternating between 29 and 30 days.

The problem with these lunar calendars is that keeping time with the moon is about as reliable as a flaky friend. That's because the revolution of the moon around the earth has no relation to earth's journey around the sun (which takes about 365.25 days). The Muslim and Hebrew calendars—lunar calendars similar to

5

What is the the present-day name for the star the Egyptians called Sothis?

those of the Ancient Egyptians and Babylonians—both contained 354 days, which meant the first day of these calendars actually occurred at a different time of the year each year. To solve this problem, the Hebrew calendar added an extra month every second or third year. Kind of like a leap month!

Around 3000 BCE, the Egyptians noticed that the star Sothis—what we call "Sirius" or the "Dog Star"—rose next to the sun every 365 days. This happened just before the annual flooding of the Nile, so the Egyptians realized that their lunar calendar wasn't quite right. To fix this, they added five extra days to the end of the year, five days that didn't belong to any month, to create a more accurate 365-day calendar.

In later years, Egyptians explained the origin of the five epagomenal days—that is, "days outside the calendar"—by saying that the god Thoth won them in a dice game played against the moon. Too bad Thoth couldn't try his luck at Vegas!

Making Our Modern Calendar

The calendar we use today seems especially stable—30 days has September, April, June, and November—but creating that calendar took a lot of work.

Around 750 BCE, Romulus, the founder of Rome, is believed to have created a 10-month calendar, which included six months of 30 days (April, June, Sextilis, September, November, and December) and four months of 31 days (March, May, Quinctilis, and October). A few minutes with a calculator tells us this year had only 304 days—far too short! The second king of Rome, Numa Pompilius, tried to correct the problem by adding January to the beginning of the year and February to the end. February was later moved to follow January, and the lengths of the months were changed so that half had 29 days and half had 30. Now we're getting

WORDS TO KNOW

epagomenal days: *days outside of the regular Egyptian calendar.*

tzolkin: *a Mayan calendar consisting of 260 days.*

6

Who was the second king of Rome?

A DIFFERENT KIND OF CALENDAR

Today almost every calendar is based on how long the earth takes to revolve around the sun, but that wasn't always the case. The Mayan civilization, which lasted for about 4,000 years in Central America, kept two calendars. One was the standard 365-day solar calendar, called haab; the other was a 260-day calendar called tzolkin, or the "count of the days."

The tzolkin was based partly on the movement of the planet Venus, but the number 260 was also important because that's about how many days pass between a woman getting pregnant and giving birth. Also, 260 is the number you get when you multiply the number of digits on a human's hands and feet (20) with the number of layers in Mayan heaven (13).

The Mayans used their two calendars at the same time, and together these calendars created a cycle of 18,980 days. This 52-year-long cycle—just about how long humans lived at the time—was celebrated by Aztec priests with a trek to the Hill of the Star near Mexico City, where they watched for special signs from the heavens.

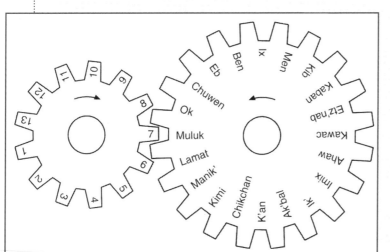

These gears—one with 13 notches, the other with 20—can represent the passing of days on the tzolkin. Just as Monday might be the 2nd one month and the 5th the next, Muluk will be the 7th one time and the 1st the next time around. When Muluk is again the 7th, one 260-day cycle will be complete.

The 260-day calendar called tzolkin.

7

How many months did the Roman calendar first have around the year 750 BCE? How many days?

You can still see signs of the old Roman calendar in the months September, October, November, and December. Sept-, oct-, non-, and deca- are prefixes based on the Latin and Greek words for seven, eight, nine, and ten. Think of the eight-legged octopus, for example, or the decathalon, a track-and-field event with ten parts. November used to be the ninth month, but when Julius moved January and February, the "novem" part no longer made sense. To match the new calendar, we should really celebrate Thanksgiving in Hendecember!

Hendecember

SUNDAY	MONDAY	TUESDAY	WEDNESDAY	THURSDAY	FRIDAY	SATURDAY
1	2	3	4	5	6	7
8	9	10	11	12	13	14
15	16	17	18	19	20	21
22	23	24	25	26	27	28
29	30					

closer—354 days. Since Romans thought even numbers were unlucky, they added an extra day to make the calendar 355 days long.

As the years passed, the Romans realized that their calendar was *still* too short. To solve the problem, they added the month of Mercedinus (lasting either 22 or 23 days) to the calendar every other year between the 23rd and 24th of February. So over a four-year period, the Romans had years lasting 355, 378, 355, and 379 days. Quite complicated!

Why did the Romans create an appearing and disappearing month instead of merely adding 10 days to the calendar? No one knows, but most likely tradition won out over common sense. We could ask ourselves similar questions: Why do we use a 60-second minute and a 60-minute hour when we count almost everything else by tens? Why 24 hours in a day and not 20 or 30? The answer in each case is tradition. It's almost always easier to do what's familiar than switch to something new.

In Rome the month of Mercedinus lasts 22 days; or is it 23 days? The year lasts 355 days. No wait, it lasts 378 days; or was it 355? No, it was 379 days.

Luckily for us, Julius Caesar was willing to risk something new. When he came to power in 46 BCE,

Julius Caesar

What were the names of the months we now call July and August?

he found that previous government officials had manipulated the calendar so many times that the Roman calendar was 90 days off from the actual seasons. To get the calendar back on track, Julius declared that the current year (45 BCE) would last 445 days instead of 355; January and February would now be the first two months of the year instead of the last; and months would last either 30 or 31 days, except for February, which would have 29 days most of the time and 30 days every fourth year.

To honor Julius, the Roman senate took the month of Quintilis and renamed it July. In 8 BCE, the senate made Sextilis into August to similarly honor Augustus Caesar. At the same time, they stole a day from February to make August last as long as July. A good idea since Augustus was still in charge at the time!

This revised Julian calendar was almost a match with the length of a solar year—but as we've all learned from math and spelling tests, almost isn't good enough. The calendar was 11 minutes and 14 seconds too long. Eleven minutes might not seem like much, but in 400 years that extra time adds up to three days.

By the year 1582, the spring equinox (the day when the number of hours of daylight and nighttime are equal—also called the vernal equinox) had moved forward 10 days, from March 21 to March 11. This upset the Christian church since the date of Easter each year had been defined as the first Sunday after the first full moon after the spring equinox. If something wasn't done, Easter would eventually fall on the same day as Christmas.

WORDS TO KNOW

Julian calendar: *calendar created by Julius Caesar in 45 BCE.*

equinox: *the day in spring (March 20, 21, or 22) or fall (September 20, 21, or 22) when the number of hours of daylight and nighttime are equal and the sun rises directly in the east and sets directly in the west.*

On what date did the spring equinox fall in the year 1582?

As Julius Caesar did more than 1,600 years earlier, Pope Gregory XIII decided to change the length of the year just once to get the calendar back on track. He decreed that October 4 would be followed immediately by October 15. Furthermore, instead of having a leap year every four years, years divisible by 100 (but not 400) would not contain an extra day. This change takes care of the 11 extra minutes

Pope Gregory XIII

CALENDAR CALCULATORS

Abbé Marco Mastrofini, an Italian priest who lived from 1763 to 1845, was a professor of philosophy and mathematics. He was best known during his life for his writings on usury, which is another term for interest charged on a loan. Of most interest to us, though, is his work on calendar reform. Mastrofini was bothered by the way the dates shifted throughout the years and wanted to offer a way to keep the days and dates the same from year to year.

Although Mastrofini never saw his revised Gregorian calendar put into practice, others have carried on his efforts. The best known supporter of Mastrofini's World Calendar must be Elisabeth Achelis, who founded the World Calendar Association in 1930 in New York. For decades, Achelis pushed the United Nations to adopt the World Calendar, and to this day the International World Calendar Association still champions the cause of calendar reform.

WORDS TO KNOW

Gregorian calendar: *the calendar revised by Pope Gregory XIII in 1582, still in use today.*

winter solstice: *the date with the shortest day and the longest night of the year. This is December 21 or 22 in the Northern Hemisphere; June 21 or 22 in the Southern Hemisphere.*

summer solstice: *the date with the longest day and the shortest night of the year. This is June 21 or 22 in the Northern Hemisphere; December 21 or 22 in the Southern Hemisphere.*

Northern Hemisphere: *north of the equator.*

Southern Hemisphere: *south of the equator.*

equator: *line around the middle of the earth that is in between the North and South Poles.*

CALENDARIVM
GREGORIANVM
PERPETVVM.

Orbi Chriſtiano vniuerſo à GREGORIO XIII. P. M. pro-
poſitum. Anno M. D. LXXXII.

GREGORIVS EPISCOPVS
SERVVS SERVORVM DEI
AD PERPETVAM REI MEMORIAM.

each year that Julius tried to hide in the basement. The Gregorian calendar, as it's now known, will prevent the solar year from shifting again in the future.

Or will it? In fact, the Gregorian calendar contains two-and-a-half extra days over a 10,000-year period. Thankfully, we can let our great-great-great-great-great-great-great-(repeat this a hundred times)-great-grandchildren worry about this when they're rocketing from planet to planet in their personalized spaceships. For the next 2,000 years or so, we're all set.

ACTIVITY

Reading Seasons From a Shadow

Each day the sun moves across the sky from east to west (actually the sun stays in place and the earth rotates on its axis, but we can turn a blind eye to the truth for this activity). Although at first glance the sun may appear to rise from and fall to the same spot on the horizon each day, the path it takes varies over the course of the year.

The earth—and not the oh-so-much-larger sun—is once again to blame for this movement. The earth's axis is tilted at an angle of 23.5 degrees, so as the earth revolves around the sun, the part of the earth's surface that's closest to the sun changes each day.

The Northern Hemisphere tilts toward the sun in summer and away from the sun in winter.

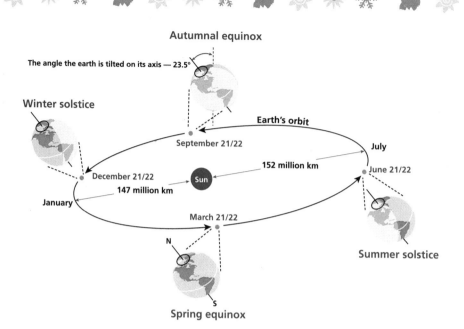

Over the course of a year, you can indirectly observe the changing arc of the sun and even discover which season it is (in case you don't have a calendar handy) by tracking the movement of shadows across the ground.

For this activity, all you need is a handful of pebbles and a straight stick, telephone pole, or flagpole stuck in the ground. On a sunny day, go out early in the morning and place a pebble (or other heavy object that won't blow away) at the end of the stick's shadow. Every hour or so throughout the day, place another pebble to mark the end of the shadow; make sure to place a pebble at noon when the shadow is at its shortest. Another word for noon is meridian, and when the sun is at its zenith—that is, directly overhead—we can say that the sun is crossing the day's meridian.

At day's end, what shape does your row of pebbles form? If it's an arc that curves toward the stick, then you know the season is summer; if the arc curves away from the pole, it's winter; if the row of pebbles forms a straight line, then

During which month is the earth closest to the sun?

it's either spring or autumn. To find out which, create a new line of pebbles one day each week until the line bends either toward or away from the stick.

This experiment will work in many locations in the Northern and Southern Hemispheres, but not on or near the equator. In these parts of the world, the sun passes directly overhead twice a year, and the sun's shadow will pass right through the stick. In June, the shadow will arc to the south because the sun is north of the equator; in December, the shadow will arc the other way.

If, however, you live way up in Alaska you'll have a different kind of surprise come summer. Because of the tilting of the earth's axis, the sun is above the horizon 24 hours a day, which means the end of the stick's shadow will actually trace out a circle. Make sure you have plenty of pebbles on hand!

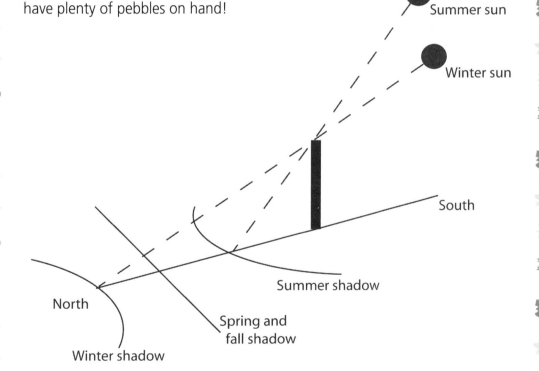

IS A BETTER CALENDAR POSSIBLE?

While Pope Gregory succeeded in matching the calendar with the solar year, not everyone was happy with the change, especially since the correction "wiped out" 10 days from the year 1582. Some countries started using the Gregorian calendar right away, but England and the American colonies adopted it only in 1752, almost two hundred years later. Japan accepted it in 1873, and China didn't switch over until 1949!

The Gregorian calendar is now used for business purposes around the world, yet problems still remain. Most businesses and governments issue reports every three months, for example, but the first quarter of the year (January, February, March) has 90 or 91 days, the second quarter has 91 days, and the final two quarters have 92. The different lengths can make it hard to compare reports from one quarter to the next.

Another sore point is that dates don't match the same day of the week from one year to the next. If the Fourth of July is on a Monday this year, next year it will be on Tuesday, and the year after that Wednesday—

unless it's a leap year in which case it will be on Thursday!

Many people have offered new calendars that avoid these problems. The most well known was created in 1834 by Marco Mastrofini. Under his proposal, each quarter would have 91 days, with a month of 31 days being followed by two months of 30 days. Since 7 divides evenly into 91, each date would always fall on the same day of the week.

Four quarters of 91 days adds up to only 364, so Mastrofini included World Day, a special holiday that would come between December 30 and January 1. Leap Day would come after June 30 every fourth year. Both World Day and Leap Day would be holidays and not associated with Monday, Tuesday, or any other day.

Many organizations support this World Calendar, and even the United Nations has considered adopting it, but it's unlikely to replace the Gregorian calendar we've used for the past 400 years. After all, think of how many airplane schedules, school records, tax reports, appointment books, business receipts, and millions of other documents would have to be changed!

How many days would February have using Mastrofini's "World Calendar?"

HERE COME THE HOURS

Calendars are a good starting point for tracking time, but where do we go from there? Days are easy to track, after all. The sun comes up (way too early in the morning for some night owls), the sun goes down, the sun comes up again, and on and on for millions of years. As day follows day, we group them into weeks, months, and years so that we can easily compare one length of time with another.

Going in the other direction—breaking a day into smaller pieces as opposed to stacking them up like blocks—is more complicated. Sure, a day clearly has two periods: daytime, when the sun is above the horizon, and nighttime, when it's not.

But how did we get from day and night to 24 hours? And from there to an hour of 60 minutes, each of which contains 60 seconds? As with

Make your own shadow clock

Track time like an Egyptian

Make a quadrant to find your latitude

Create a sundial for your longitude

Babylonians Discover Minutes and Seconds

The Ancient Times Herald

Egyptians Divide Night into 12 Equal Parts

Equal Rights Group Insists Day Must Get Same Treatment

Lorem ipsum dolor sit amet, conse ctetuer adipiscing elit, sed diam no nummy nibh euismod tincidunt ut la oreet dolore magna aliquam erat vo lutpat. Ut wisi enim ad minim venia m, quis nostrud exerci tation ullamc

Lorem ipsum dolor sit amet, conse ctetuer adipiscing elit, sed diam no nummy nibh euismod tincidunt ut la oreet dolore magna aliquam erat vo lutpat. Ut wisi enim ad minim venia m, quis nostrud exerci tation ullamc

the creation of calendars, we have to give credit to the Ancient Egyptians and the Babylonians.

As you might remember from the first chapter, the Egyptians created a 365-day calendar only after noticing that once every 365 days the star Sothis rose in the sky just before the sun did. Having only one star to set your watch by is hardly enough though, so the Egyptians identified 35 other stars and constellations that rose during daylight just like Sothis.

They used the rising of these stars as the starting point for each of their 10-day-long weeks. By watching these stars, Egyptians were able to keep their calendar on track.

In addition to rising in daylight, these stars were visible at night, of course, rising over the horizon at regular intervals as the earth turned. Using the nighttime travel of these stars as a guideline, the Egyptians divided the night into 12 equal parts. Since night and day last about the same length of time, Egyptians decided to divide daytime into 12 parts, too. And that is how the 24-hour day was born.

Egyptian Star Calendar.

To track the 12 daytime hours, Egyptians used a shadow clock, which is also known as a time stick. Shadow clocks are one of the oldest ways to measure time by the movement of the sun. Archeologists have found shadow clocks

WORDS TO KNOW

constellation: *group of stars.*

shadow clock: *a clock developed by Ancient Egyptians that used the sun's shadow to track time.*

How many days were in the Egyptian week?

dating back more than 3,500 years, but simple ones were probably used even earlier—a stick stuck in the ground was most likely the first such sun clock.

Making Minutes

Like the Egyptians, the Babylonians used the movement of the stars to divide both day and night into 12 equal parts. But the Babylonians, who had already made great advances in arithmetic, went even further by dividing each hour into 60 pieces (minutes), and each of those pieces into 60 even smaller parts (seconds).

Egyptians ask "How many parts does a day need anyway?"

The **Ancient Times Herald**

Babylonians Invent Minutes and Seconds

"Base 60" math system really catches on

Lorem ipsum dolor sit amet, conse ctetuer adipiscing elit, sed diam no nummy nibh euismod tincidunt ut la oreet dolore magna aliquam erat vo lutpat. Ut wisi enim ad minim venia m, quis nostrud exerci tation ullamc

Lorem ipsum dolor sit amet, conse ctetuer adipiscing elit, sed diam no nummy nibh euismod tincidunt ut la oreet dolore magna aliquam erat vo lutpat. Ut wisi enim ad minim venia m, quis nostrud exerci tation ullamc

Why 60? Hard to say. Most people today count by groups of tens, so, for example, the number 458 is made up of eight single units, five groups of 10 single units, and four groups of 100 single units (that is, 10 tens). Mathematicians call this

---

MIDDLE EASTERN MONARCHS

When Alexander the Great died in 323 BCE, the generals in his army divided up his empire. General Seleucus became king of the eastern part of the empire that included Iran, Iraq, Syria, and Afghanistan. Seleucids and Greeks traded with each other, which helped each culture stay aware of the scientific advances of the other. In addition to giving us the base 60 counting system, the Seleucid dynasty is thought to have been the first in the Middle East that kept a continuous record of years as they passed. Before Seleucus took over, these countries tracked years only by referring to who ruled the country at that time. You might say that you were born during the "fifth year of Darius," for example, and everyone who lived in the same area would know what you meant. However, anyone outside the country would be confused and not know how old you were. What if your mother said she was born in the "second year of Ford?" Does this make it easier or harder to know how old she is?

ACTIVITY

Tracking Hours Like an Egyptian

To make your own shadow clock you will need:

• a piece of wood that is 20 inches long, 2 inches wide, and 1 inch thick

• a piece of wood that is 17 inches long, 2 inches wide, and 1 inch thick

• a piece of wood that is 3 inches long, 2 inches wide, and 1 inch thick

• several small nails

• light- and dark-colored paint

Believe it or not you'll also need a **watch**; Egyptians didn't have watches, of course, but we're taking a shortcut for the moment.

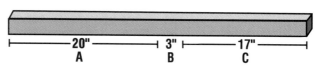

First, nail the three sections of wood together as shown in the illustration. Paint the time stick a light color so that you'll be able to see shadows on it easily.

At 7:00 in the morning on a sunny day, take the time stick outside and place it on the ground with the back of the top bar facing east—that is, toward the sun. To make sure the time stick is level, fill a glass with water, place it on the stick, and adjust the stick until the water in the glass is level. (You could also use a carpenter's level, but learning how to level something the old-school way is a neat trick.)

Chapter Two: Here Come the Hours

Use the dark paint or a pencil to mark where the shadow of the bar falls on the stick. The bar is an example of a gnomon (pronounced NO-mon), a vertical device that casts a shadow on some sort of ruler or measuring stick to keep track of time.

Go outside each hour from 8 am to 11 am, and mark the shadow on the stick. At noon, turn the time stick around so that the back of the top bar faces west. When the shadow of the bar reaches the mark you made at 11 am, the time will now be 1 pm. As the day goes on, the shadows will mark the hours from 2 pm to 5 pm. The five marks on your shadow clock divide the day into six hours before noon and six hours after, so now you can track time like an Egyptian!

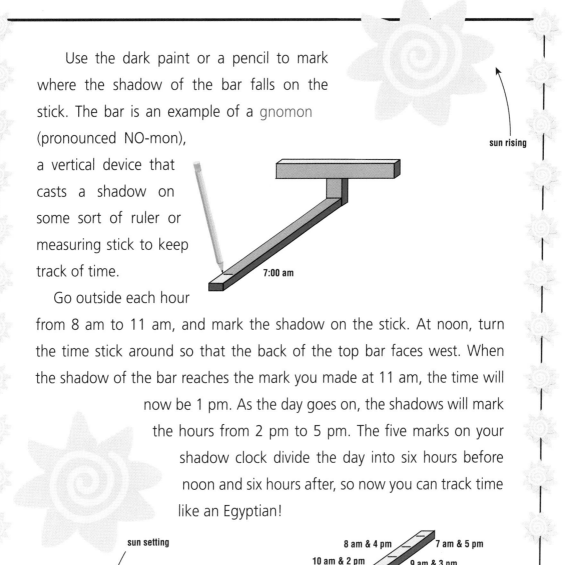

WORDS TO KNOW

gnomon: *a vertical device that casts a shadow on a measuring stick to track of time.*

base 10 counting system: *a number system based on units of 10.*

base 60 counting system: *a number system based on units of 60.*

type of number system a base 10 system. The Babylonians counted by tens, but they also had counting systems based on 2, 4, 12, 24, and—you guessed it—60.

In a base 60 counting system, based on units of 60, the units column goes from 0 to 59 and then rolls over to 0 as the sixties column changes from 0 to 1. You've probably seen the numbers roll over a hundred times on an electronic digital clock, but never thought about it before in terms of a base 60 counting system. You know more math than you realize!

The base 60 counting system was in place by the time of the Seleucid dynasty, which started after the death of Alexander the Great in 323 BCE and included the city of Babylon. The Greeks adopted the Babylonian timekeeping system and later passed it on to the Romans, who spread it throughout Europe.

Shadows in Your Neighborhood

Shadow clocks are a good first attempt at timekeeping, but they really aren't very accurate. As the activity in chapter one showed, a gnomon's shadow changes its path and length throughout the year, so a time stick created in summer will have different markings from one made in winter.

The Egyptians were okay with "hours" in the summer lasting longer than "hours" in the winter. Daylight lasted longer in summer than in winter, so for them it was only natural that summer hours be longer. In fact, when they invented other timekeeping devices later, they made sure to use different hour marks during different parts of the year to keep track of the hours properly. We'll talk more about these clocks in chapter three.

Hours that grow and shrink may have been fine for the Egyptians, but later civilizations wanted an hour to mean the same thing throughout the year. The Greek inventor Anaximander (611-546 BCE) has been credited with creating the sundial, which is a more complex—and more accurate—version of the shadow clock.

Instead of measuring time by how long the gnomon's shadow is (as shadow clocks do), sundials measure time

20

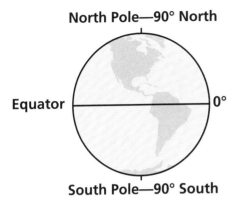

North Pole—90° North

Equator   **0°**

South Pole—90° South

by tracking which direction the shadow points. By design, the shadow of a sundial's gnomon should point in the same direction at the same time of day throughout the year. Whether it's January or July, when it's one hour past the sun's highest point in the sky, the shadow should fall on 1:00. *Should* fall, mind you, but it's not guaranteed.

Here's how the hour indicated by the gnomon's shadow depends on three things: the angle of the gnomon, the direction the gnomon faces, and the layout of the hour markers on the face of the sundial. A gnomon that rises off the sundial at an

A MAN AHEAD OF HIS TIME

Little is known about Anaximander, the inventor of the sundial, but what we do know makes him sound a bit like a modern scientist.

For example, Anaximander thought that before anything else existed, there was only apeiron, *a Greek word that means an unending, unlimited mass. Explosions in this apeiron flung material out into the universe—much like our current view of the Big Bang—and worlds formed from this material, with the heavier substances like rock sinking to the middle of these objects.*

Anaximander differed from modern scientists, however, in thinking that the earth was shaped like a cylinder and the stars were fixed on a sphere that rotated around earth.

Like modern scientists, Anaximander thought that all living organisms developed in water and only later moved onto land. Unlike today's scientists, he thought that all sea animals developed in husks or shells and only lost the shells once they left the ocean.

80-degree angle will make a different shadow than one angled at 20 degrees, or even 70 degrees. If the tip of the gnomon points northeast, it will make different shadows from one pointing north. And, obviously, you can't place the hour markers just anywhere; you need to know enough about the sun's movement that the shadows will fall where they should.

The Greek astronomer, Ptolemy

To solve these problems, you need to design the sundial and its gnomon based upon your latitude. Latitude is a measure of how far north or south of the equator you are located. The equator is a line around the middle of the earth that's equally far from the North and South Poles. The Greek astronomer Ptolemy set the equator as 0 degrees latitude, the North Pole as 90 degrees latitude north, and the South Pole as 90 degrees latitude south.

Why 90? Again, we have the Babylonians to thank. When the Babylonians still considered one year to equal 360 days, they divided circles into 360 sections since years and circles have much in common. Just as you would see the same objects again and again if you walked only in a circle, the seasons follow each other the same way year after year. Today, we call the sections of a circle "degrees." The North Pole is one-quarter of a circle away from the equator, and one-quarter of 360 degrees is 90.

90°

90°

0°
360°

90°

WORDS TO KNOW:

degrees: *a measure for arcs and angles; sections of a circle.*

latitude: *a measure of how far north or south of the equator you are located.*

Sun's rays—hitting earth at different angles

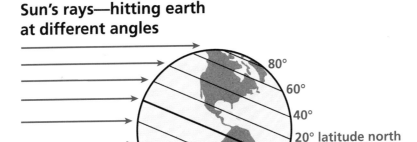

For each degree of latitude, the sun's rays hit the earth at a different angle. On March 21, the sun is directly over the equator so its rays hit the earth at a 90 degree angle (which is also called a right angle). If you live in Houston, Texas (which has a latitude around 30 degrees north), the sun shines down at a 60-degree angle; if you live in Anchorage, Alaska, the sun shines at a 30-degree angle, because Anchorage lies at 60 degrees latitude north. And at the North Pole, the sun will barely be over the horizon, with its rays almost parallel to the ground.

Because the angle of the sun's rays is based upon your latitude, you need a sundial designed specifically for your area. Otherwise the sundial won't be reliable. You can find your latitude a number of ways, some easy and some not so easy. The easiest way is to use information from the U.S. Geological Survey, which is available at libraries and online at http://geonames.usgs.gov/. Choose the U.S. and territories query, and select your state. To get more specific, type the name of your town into the "feature name" window. The hardest way would be to travel to the equator, walk directly north until you reach your hometown—counting your steps on the way—then convert your step count into miles and finally latitude.

Another way is to use a sextant, a tool that sailors can use to help them know where they are on the ocean. A sextant measures the angle between two objects, and you can make a simple sextant, called a quadrant, that will determine your latitude so that you can build an accurate sundial.

Which ancient astronomer set the degrees latitude for the equator and North and South Poles?

Finding Your Latitude

To make a navigator's quadrant, you will need:

- a protractor (a tool that helps you draw angles on paper)
- a clear straw
- tape
- a foot of string
- a jumbo paper clip or other small object

Tape the straw to the protractor so that the straw lies across the center mark and the 90-degree mark. Tie the string to the paper clip, then tape the string to the center mark of the protractor. (If you hold the protractor straight up and down with the straw parallel to the ground, the string should pass through the 0-degree mark.)

To use the quadrant, hold it so that the rounded part of the protractor faces down. Look through the straw at some object, such as the top of a building or a tree, and hold the protractor steady. When the string stops swinging, hold it against the protractor and see where it falls on the scale from 0–90 degrees. If, for example, the string lies on 37, then you know that the top of the building is at a 37-degree angle from the ground where you are currently standing.

To find your latitude, go outside at night and locate the Big Dipper overhead. Use the pointer stars on the cup of the Big Dipper to find Polaris. Polaris is also known as the North Star because it lies directly over the North Pole. Look through your quadrant at Polaris and find the angle of Polaris over the horizon. This number also equals your latitude!

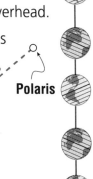

Polaris

37°

line of sight

Ursa Minor
"Little Dipper"

Polaris

Ursa Major
"Big Dipper"

ACTIVITY

Build Your Own Sundial

Once you have found your latitude, you can create a sundial perfect for your neck of the woods. To make a sundial you will need:

- a ruler
- a pencil
- thick white paper
- a protractor (without the straw taped to it)

1. Draw line **AB**, and mark the center of line **AB** with the point **O**. (This line will be the six o'clock line in the finished drawing, so you can place it near the bottom of the page.)

A•————————————O————————————•B

2. At a right angle (90 degrees) to line **AB**, draw line **CO**. (This will be the twelve o'clock line.)

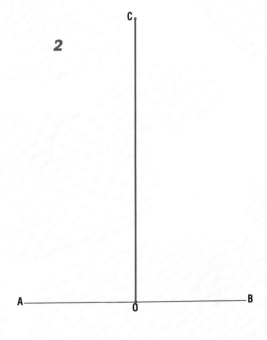

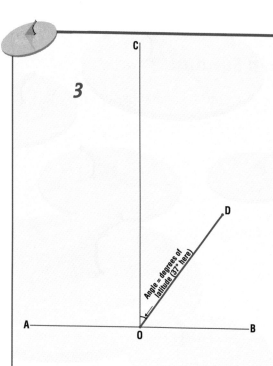

3

Angle = degrees of latitude (37° here)

3. Draw line **OD**. The angle **COD** must be equal in degrees to your latitude. Use the protractor by placing it with the O-degree mark on line **CO** and the 90-degree mark on line **AB**. If your latitude is, for example, 37 degrees, then make a mark at 37 on the protractor. Then use the ruler to draw a straight line from **O** through this mark.

4. Somewhere along the line **OD**, mark a point **E**. (Where you place **E** will determine how large the finished sundial is. If **E** is four inches from **O**, then the finished diagram will be roughly seven inches by eight inches.)

5. From point **E**, draw a line at a right angle to **OD** until it hits line **CO**. Mark the intersection as point **F**.

4 & 5

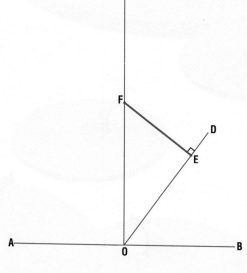

6. Measure the distance from **E** to **F**, then mark point **G** on the line **CO** so that the distance between **F** and **G** is the same as between **E** and **F**.

7. Through point **F**, draw the line **QR**, making it parallel to **AB**. (Use the ruler to make sure the lines are parallel.)

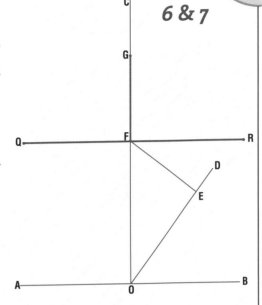

6 & 7

8 & 9

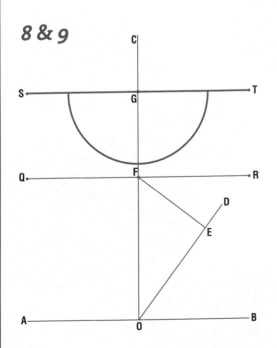

8. Through point **G**, draw the line **ST**, making it parallel to **AB** and **QR**.

9. Using the protractor, draw a semicircle that begins and ends on line **ST** with point **G** as its center. (The semicircle can be any size as long as it doesn't go below line **QR**.)

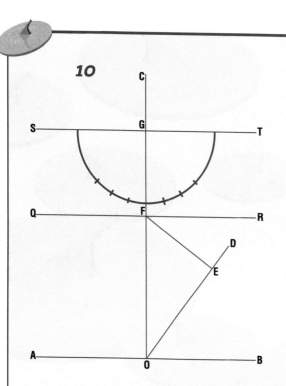

10

10. With the protractor still centered on point **G**, make three marks, 15 degrees apart, to the left and the right of **GF**.

11. Using the ruler, draw straight lines from point **G** through each of these six marks to line **QR**. You now have seven points on line **QR** (including point **F**). Label these points from left to right with the hours **9**, **10**, **11**, **12**, **1**, **2**, and **3**.

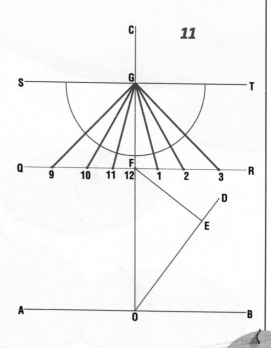

11

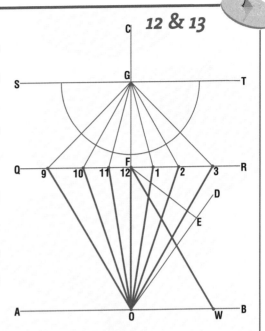

12 & 13

12. Using the ruler, from point **O** draw straight lines connecting **O** with the points labeled **9**, **10**, **11**, **1**, **2**, and **3**. These will be the hour lines on the finished sundial.

13. From point **F**, draw a line parallel to the line going from point **O** to **9**. Make this line go all the way to line **AB** and label the point where the lines intersect point **W**.

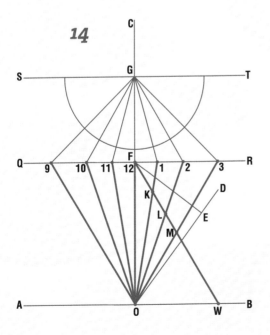

14

14. Where the line **FW** crosses the one, two, and three o'clock lines, mark the points **K**, **L**, and **M**.

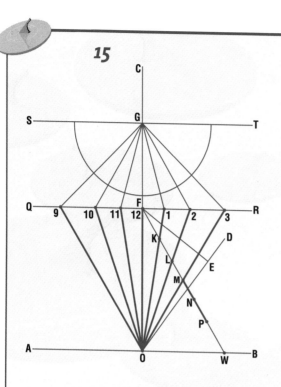

15

15. On the line **FW**, you will now mark the points **N** and **P**. The distance between **M** and **N** must be the same as the distance between **L** and **M**. Measure this distance with the ruler, then mark point **N**. The distance between **M** and **P** must be the same as the distance between **K** and **M**. Measure this distance, then mark point **P**.

16. Using the ruler, draw two lines parallel to line **FO**. One line will connect the point labeled **9** with the line **AB**, and the other line will connect the point labeled **3** with the line **AB**. (This line should pass through point **W**.)

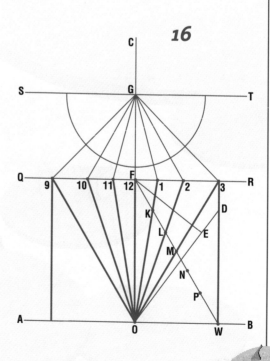

16

17 & 18

17. Using the ruler, draw lines from point **O** through points **N** and **P** until you hit the line going from **3** to point **W**. These lines are the four and five o'clock lines so mark them **4** and **5** on the line going from **3** to point **W**.

18. On the line going from **9** to line **AB**, mark the points **7** and **8**. The distance between **7** and **9** must be the same as the distance between

3 and **5**. Similarly, the distance between **8** and **9** must match the distance between **3** and **4**.

19 & 20

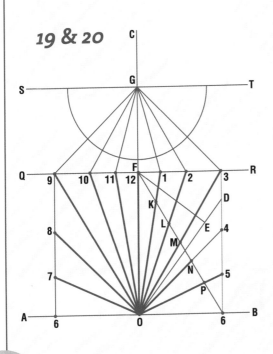

19. Draw lines from point **O** to the **7** and point **O** to the **8**. These lines are the seven and eight o'clock lines.

20. Change point **W** to point **6** and where **9** crosses the line **AB** also mark point **6**.

21. Stand back and admire your completed diagram!

Note that this diagram works only for those living in the Northern Hemisphere. Anyone living in the Southern Hemisphere must reverse the order of the hour markers, so that the digits across the line **QR** read "**3, 2, 1, 12, 11, 10, 9**." Change points **7** and **8** to **5** and **4**, and **5** and **4** to **7** and **8**. Your sundial will be "upside-down" compared to those in the Northern Hemisphere, and reversing the numbers will make the sundial work properly.

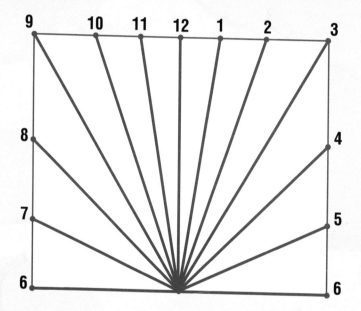

This drawing might look a bit messy since you had to draw so many lines other than the hour lines. You can erase all the extra lines, or you can place another sheet of paper on top of this one and trace only the hour lines onto this new sheet. Before you erase everything, though, use this drawing to help draw your gnomon. After all, without the gnomon your sundial isn't going to be very useful!

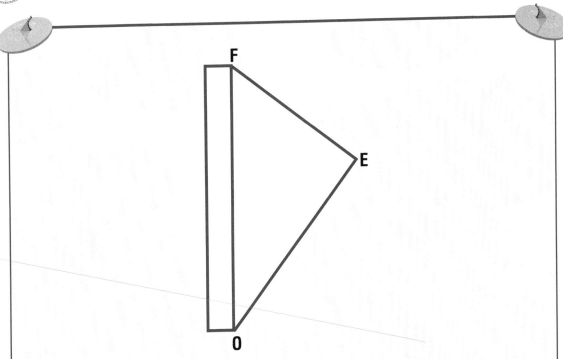

The gnomon must be the same size and have the same angle as lines **OF** and **OE** in your sundial drawing. Either trace the triangle **FOE** onto a separate sheet of thick paper, or repeat steps 1–5 (making everything the same length as before) until you have drawn triangle **FOE**. Draw a long skinny rectangle next to line **OF**; this rectangle will fit inside a slot you make along the twelve o'clock line on your sundial so that the gnomon can stand upright. Place the gnomon so that point **F** on the gnomon lies at point **O** on the sundial, then tape or glue the pieces together.

You can glue the sundial to wood or cardboard to make it sturdier. Then place it outside with the twelve o'clock line pointing exactly north. (Use a compass to find which direction is north, or wait until noon and position the sundial so that the gnomon doesn't create a shadow.) Use a glass of water or a carpenter's level to make sure the sundial is level.

If you've positioned everything correctly, the gnomon will point directly at Polaris!

Why You Shouldn't Use a Sundial

After all that hard work you might be surprised to learn that sundials aren't very useful in today's society. While a sundial can tell you the time at your exact location, that time might not match the clock on your wall. Why not? Because the United States—and almost every other country in the world—uses time zones. We'll talk about time zones a lot more in chapter seven.

Within a time zone the hour and minutes are always the same. The Eastern time zone, for example, stretches all the way from Maine to Indiana, so clocks in Portland and Indianapolis will always match.

But if you take a walk outside, you'll see the sun (and sundials) don't work the same way. Because of the rotation of the earth, the sun will be directly overhead in Portland long before it's overhead in Indianapolis. This means that a sundial in Portland might say the time is noon and a sundial in Indianapolis might say it's 11:15—while the clocks in both towns say it's actually 11:38!

TELLING TIME AFTER TWILIGHT

Shadow clocks and sundials are extremely useful timekeeping devices—except, of course, on cloudy days, or during the night, or in the middle of a thunderstorm, or during a sandstorm, or . . .

Okay, so maybe timekeeping devices that rely on the sun aren't always the best idea. The Ancient Egyptians realized this, too, so to track time when the sun wasn't visible overhead, the Egyptians turned away from the heavens and used a more down-to-earth substance: water. The klepsydra—named for the Greek words for "water thief"—is a clock made from water and a bucket.

Sound confusing? Here's the idea: Make a small hole in the bottom of a bucket, then plug the hole with clay or plastic. Fill the bucket with water and mark

Make your own klepsydra and measure time using water

Meet the inventors of the greatest water clocks ever invented

Make your own nocturnal and tell time by the stars

WORDS TO KNOW

klepsydra: *A clock that uses dripping water to track time. Also called a water glass.*

Sports News - Chariot Races Tomorrow. Attendance numbers down at Olympics

The **Ancient Times Herald**

Clever Egyptians Use Water to Track Time
The Klepsydra — The Future of Timekeeping

Socrates Dies
Final words were,
"I Drank What?"

Lorem ipsum dolor sit amet, conse ctetuer adipiscing elit, sed diam no nummy nibh euismod tincidunt ut la oreet dolore magna aliquam erat vo lutpat. Ut wisi enim ad minim venia m, quis nostrud exerci tation ullamc orper suscipit lobortis nisl ut aliquip

ACTIVITY

Watching the Hours Flow By

You can make a simple klepsydra of your own, but instead of marking the bucket that water flows out of, you'll mark the container that water flows into. For this project, you need to gather the following materials:

- a quart-sized tin can, such as a large coffee can
- acrylic paint
- a needle
- a hammer
- nails
- two pieces of wood 9.5 inches long and 4.5 inches wide
- three pieces of wood 5 inches long and 1.5 inches wide
- a quart-sized glass jar, such as one used for mayonnaise or pickles

Paint the tin can with acrylic paint both inside and out to help keep it from rusting. Use the hammer and needle to poke a very small hole in the bottom of the can. (If the hole turns out to be too large, cover the hole with electrical tape or duct tape and poke another smaller hole.)

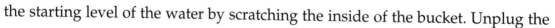

the starting level of the water by scratching the inside of the bucket. Unplug the hole to start the water flowing, then use a shadow clock (or watch) to track the hours. Mark the current water level as each hour passes. Don't mark the actual hour of the day; instead mark the hours one, two, three, and so forth because the klepsydra measures hours only from when you start the water flowing, which could be at any time during the day.

Once the bucket is empty, you'll know how many hours you can track with this particular klepsydra. A klepsydra made by someone else might track time differently because

Klepsydra.

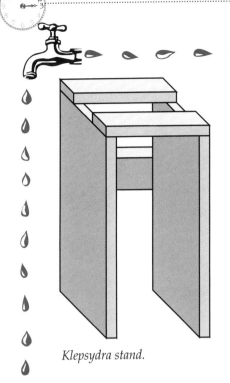

Klepsydra stand.

Nail the small strips of wood to the large ones as shown in the diagram to create a stand for the tin can. Place the glass jar underneath the stand, fill the tin can with water, and place the can on the stand so that the water drains into the glass jar. As each hour passes, mark the current level of the water in the glass jar—not the can—until the can is empty.

You now have a simple clock that's easy to use. If, for example, you must do two hours of homework before you can go outside and play soccer, you can fill the glass jar with water to the two-hour mark, hold your finger over the hole in the can, pour the water into the can, then let the water start flowing. As soon as the water stops dripping, you can put on your cleats and hit the playing field.

the hole on the bottom is smaller or the bucket larger, or perhaps they live in Minnesota where water doesn't run at all in the winter since it's frozen solid!

Sunny Days Make Time Pass Faster

Because water generally flows at a constant rate, an hour measured with a klepsydra will be about the same throughout the year. For Egyptians, this was a bad thing. After all, Egyptian hours weren't the same length throughout the year. When daylight lasted longer in the summer, the hours were longer as well. To make klepsydras match their hours, Egyptians used a different set of marks for each month of the year.

Why is dripping water a pretty good way to measure time?

A NEW ALARM CLOCK

With a little extra work—and very understanding parents—you can even turn your klepsydra into an alarm clock. Let's say, for example, that your bedtime is 9 pm and you have to wake up at 6 am to get ready for school. You want to set up the flow of water so that the glass jar gets full after exactly nine hours, the amount you sleep at night. At bedtime, fill the can with more water than the glass jar will hold, then arrange the whole contraption on a shelf over your head. Come 6:00 in the morning, the water will flow over the top of the jar and start dripping on your head.

Many different cultures used klepsydras all the way to the eighteenth century. As the years passed, Greek and Roman horologists (a fancy word for those who make clocks or measure time) created more complicated designs for klepsydras, such as air-filled containers that sank into the water as the hours passed. They tried to control the pressure of the water so that it flowed at a precise rate all the time. (Water flows a bit faster from a full bucket than from a nearly empty one because of the weight of the water itself.) Later, they used devices that floated on water and identified the hours by either pointing a rotating hand or ringing gongs or bells.

One of the largest examples of a water clock is the Tower of the Winds, which still stands in Athens, Greece. Andronicus, an astronomer from Macedonia, designed the Tower of the Winds (known then as

WORDS TO KNOW

horologist: *someone who makes clocks and watches.*
horology: *the art of designing and making clocks.*

the Horologion) sometime between 100 BCE and 100 CE. The Tower is 42 feet tall, 26 feet in diameter, and shaped like an octagon, with the walls facing toward the main points on a compass: north, northeast, east, and so on. Originally, the top of the Tower had a bronze figure that pointed in the direction of the wind.

The Tower of the Winds actually featured two timekeeping systems: a set of eight sundials and a 24-hour klepsydra. One sundial hung on each of the eight walls, underneath a sculpture of the figure that represented the wind that blew in that direction.

LOST IN THE WINDS

Unlike today, when we record every detail of every event so that later generations will know all about us, the Greeks were much more laid back about tracking who did what.

We know, for example, that Andronicus designed the Tower of the Winds, but we know little about Andronicus himself. He lived in Macedonia, an area north of Greece's current borders. He was possibly educated in Alexandria, according to

www.sailingissues.com

Greek scholar Hermann Kienast, because some "schools" in Alexandria specialized in the design of water clocks. (Ancient Greek schools weren't organized like schools today with different classes each hour. Think of them instead as open colleges where students studied what they wanted to when they wanted to.)

Other than those few facts—and the sturdy Tower itself—everything else known about Andronicus has been lost to the winds of history.

Who designed the Horologion? (Hint: we call this invention the Tower of the Winds.)

IMPERIAL TIMEKEEPER

Su Sung was a government administrator and a diplomat, so why did the emperor of China ask him to build a clock? Simple: in addition to being interested in science, Su Sung knew plenty of craftsmen and technicians, so he was able to bring together a team that could do the job right.

Building the water clock took at least eight years: two to build a working wooden model, two to cast the bronze parts of the clock, and four more to finish everything else. It was a lot of work, but in the end Su Sung created the best clock the world had ever seen.

And yet, within a generation, Su Sung's fabulous creation was pushed into the shadows, ignored by a government official named Wang Fu who wrote a report on astronomical water clocks. Wang Fu belonged to a different government "party" than Su Sung, and by excluding the clock from his report, Wang Fu made Su Sung look less important.

Luckily, Su Sung wrote and illustrated a book about his clock, and different copies of the book were discovered in the seventeenth, nineteenth, and twentieth centuries, letting the modern world know about this great achievement of the past.

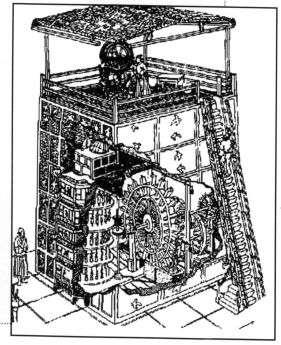

The water for the klepsydra flowed down from a reservoir on the south side of the roof. Little of the klepsydra survives today, but it seems to have been very sophisticated, with a mechanical device that displayed the hours on the outside of the Tower.

The Niagara of water clocks must surely be one created by Su Sung around 1090 CE. The Chinese began using water clocks at about the same time as the

Great Wall Construction Continues Amidst Rumours of Budget Overages

The Ancient Times Herald

Tatars Invade China—Sung Dynasty Ends

Giant Water Clock Stolen—Clues dry up

Lorem ipsum dolor sit amet, conse ctetuer adipscing elit, sed diam no nummy nibh euismod tincidunt ut la oreet dolore magna aliquam erat vo lutpat. Ut wisi enim ad minim venia m, quis nostrud exerci tation ullamc orper suscipit lobortis nisl ut aliquip ex ea commodo consequat. Duis autem vel eum iriure dolor in hendre

Lorem ipsum dolor sit amet, conse ctetuer adipscing elit, sed diam no nummy nibh euismod tincidunt ut la oreet dolore magna aliquam erat vo lutpat. Ut wisi enim ad minim venia m, quis nostrud exerci tation ullamc orper suscipit lobortis nisl ut aliquip ex ea commodo consequat. Duis autem vel eum iriure dolor in hendre

Egyptians, and between 700 and 1000 CE they began creating klepsydras that used waterwheels. Water would flow into a small bucket attached to a wheel until the bucket was so heavy that the wheel turned. A new bucket would then be filled, turning the wheel again. As the wheel rotated, it moved mechanisms that displayed the time and different astronomical events.

The emperor of the Sung Dynasty ordered Su Sung to create the greatest clock ever. His water clock ended up being over 30 feet tall, with an automatically rotating globe of the heavens and moving mannequins that rang bells and displayed tablets indicating the hours of the day. When the Tatars invaded China in 1126, ending the Sung dynasty, the clock was stolen. Nothing remains of it today.

A Timekeeper by Any Other Name

Whether you call it a sandglass or an hourglass, one thing remains the same about this shapely timekeeping device: You're probably calling it something that it's not.

Sandglass.

Yes, some sandglasses do hold an amount of sand that takes 60 minutes to flow from the top chamber to the bottom, but throughout history they've usually held powdered egg shell or marble dust. What's more, sandglasses were often designed for specific purposes, such as measuring cooking times or timing speeches. Since it's difficult to tell when, say, one-third of the sand has fallen, these sandglasses held only as much material as was needed.

The Greeks and Romans had the ability to blow glass into the shape of a modern hourglass, but there's no proof that they did. Instead, hourglasses first show up in history in fourteenth-century Italy at about the

What were hourglasses traditionally filled with?

same time that mechanical clocks were becoming a big deal.

Sandglasses proved especially useful for sailors as the rocking of a ship on waves makes a sundial or water clock useless. Sailors generally used a half-hour-long sandglass to measure the four-hour period they stood watch on deck. At the end of each half hour, the sailor on watch flipped the sandglass and rang a bell to let others know the time, ringing the bell once after the first half hour, twice after the second half hour, and so on. At eight bells—which signaled four, eight, or 12 o'clock, either am or pm—a new sailor would take over watch.

Sailors also used sandglasses to measure the speed of their ship. Until approximately the 1600s, sailors used a measuring system called, in layman's terms, "heaving the log." This system worked as follows: A sailor tied a rope to a log, threw the log into the water behind the ship, then estimated how quickly the ship moved away from the log.

A better log-based system, most likely developed by the Dutch, made use of a sandglass to get a better estimate of a ship's speed. Sailors tied knots in a rope every 48 feet (which equals eight fathoms, a common measuring unit at the time)

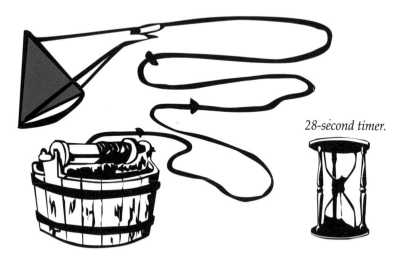

28-second timer.

Example of an early "chip log" used to measure a ship's speed.

WORDS TO KNOW

fathom: *a unit of measure equal to six feet used to measure marine depths. Comes from the old English, meaning "outstretched arms." Basically the distance between the fingers of outstretched arms.*

ACTIVITY

Make Your Own Sandglass

You don't need to be a glass blower to make your own sandglass. All it takes is:

- **two identical plastic bottles**
- **tape**
- **a piece of cardboard**
- **sand**

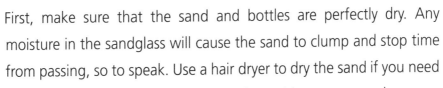

First, make sure that the sand and bottles are perfectly dry. Any moisture in the sandglass will cause the sand to clump and stop time from passing, so to speak. Use a hair dryer to dry the sand if you need to, or leave the materials outside on a sunny day.

Second, sift the sand through a sifter or some cheesecloth so that all the particles are about the same size. Again, large particles or a piece of shell could stop your sandglass from working.

Third, cut the cardboard into a circle that has the same diameter as the neck of the bottles. Make a small hole in the cardboard; you can always make the hole larger later, if you need to.

Fourth, fill one bottle half full of sand, then tape the bottle necks together with the piece of cardboard in between. Turn the bottles over, and time how long the sand takes to flow from top to bottom. Adjust the amount of sand in the bottle or the size of the hole in the cardboard so that your sandglass (or in this case "sandplastic") measures out an even amount of time. Once you're finished, it's "all aboard, matey"!

and attached the rope to a weighted log. One sailor turned over a 28-second-long sandglass, while another sailor threw the log overboard and counted how many knots were pulled overboard. When the sandglass ran out, the sailor stopped counting and reeled the log back in.

Why 28 seconds and 48 feet? If you work out the math, you'll see that the number of knots that go overboard in 28 seconds equals the number of nautical miles per hour the ship is moving. (A nautical mile measures 6,076 feet, slightly more than a mile on land.) Even though they no longer use sandglasses and logs, modern ships still measure speed in nautical miles per hour, or "knots."

Seeing Tomorrow's Stars Today

A much more complicated nighttime clock—one that dates back to at least 400 CE is the astrolabe. The astrolabe was based on the ancient Greek view of the universe, which had the earth at the center of everything and the stars in nested shells that orbited the earth.

To make an astrolabe, the Greeks flattened the three-dimensional universe to two dimensions. The North Star, Polaris, which seems not to move, was placed at the center of the astrolabe, and the Tropic of Capricorn—the name for the latitude line 23 degrees south of the equator—formed the astrolabe's outer rim. Other elements of a typical astrolabe included the 12 signs of the zodiac and a handful of the brightest stars.

By inserting a metal plate designed for a specific latitude into the astrolabe, someone using it could determine

Astrolabe.

WORDS TO KNOW

knot: *one nautical mile per hour.*

astrolabe: *a device that measures the altitude of the sun or a star to determine latitude.*

nocturnal: *a device that tells time at night using the stars.*

the time (using either equal or unequal hours) during the day or night, calculate when sunrise and sunset would happen, or find the rising or setting time of any star. It was even possible to figure out exactly how the night sky would look at any point in the past or future! Sailors used astrolabes to navigate until the eighteenth century, when it was replaced by the sextant.

STAR GAZING BY THE HOUR

Don't worry if the sun is too shy to stick around all day and light up your sundial. Just like sailors in the sixteenth and seventeenth centuries, you can use a nocturnal and turn to other stars instead.

The nocturnal was developed independently by the Spaniard, Ramon Lull, and Bernard of Verdun in the thirteenth century. Astronomers already knew that while most stars moved through the sky at night, Polaris stayed in place. Polaris lies directly over the North Pole, so as the earth spins on its axis, the position of Polaris in the sky doesn't change.

Ramon Lull and Bernard of Verdun created a device to take advantage of Polaris' reliability and the location of other stars around it. Since you must be able to see Polaris, you can use a nocturnal only if you live in the Northern Hemisphere. Even into the seventeenth century, sailors spent most of their time north of the equator, so no device similar to the nocturnal was ever created for the Southern Hemisphere.

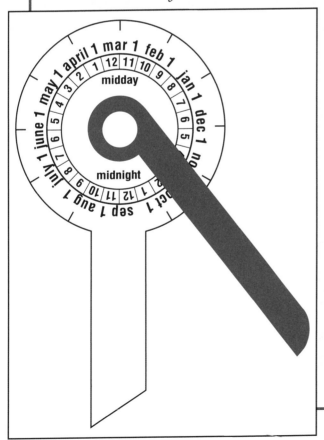

ACTIVITY

Finding Time in the Stars

Most nocturnals were made of wood or metal so that they could stand up to the soggy conditions aboard a ship. Since you're most likely living on dry land, you can use almost any sturdy material. You'll need:

• 8.5-by-11-inch piece of poster board, acrylic sheet plastic, one-eighth-inch-thick plywood, or cardboard

• a protractor

• a pen

• a threaded half-inch-long piece of pipe, and two metal nuts to fit on the pipe (the nuts must be open at both ends)

To start, draw a circle on the poster board or other material. Make the circle at least 4 inches in diameter. You can use a coffee can or bowl to draw the circle if you don't have a compass handy.

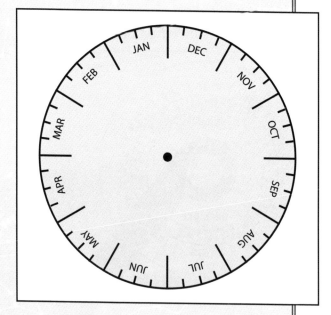

Use the protractor to divide the circle into 12 sections, with each section measuring 30 degrees. In one section, write "January," and going counterclockwise around the circle, write the names of the other 11 months. Draw three small lines in each section (at every 7.5 degrees) so that each section is divided into four smaller sections. These four smaller pieces are the weeks within each month, with the first week on the right and the last week on the left.

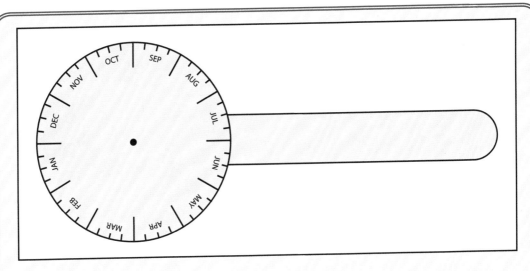

Draw a straight handle roughly 5 inches long and 1 inch wide below the June/July sections. See the picture for an example. Mark the center of the circle with a dot. Cut out the circle and its handle as one piece.

Now draw another circle that's one inch smaller in diameter than your first circle. Use the protractor to divide this circle into 24 equal sections, with each section measuring 15 degrees. Label one section "12M" for midnight, and going counterclockwise label the other hours, starting with 1 am. Draw three small lines in each hour section so that each hour is divided into four equal quarter hours.

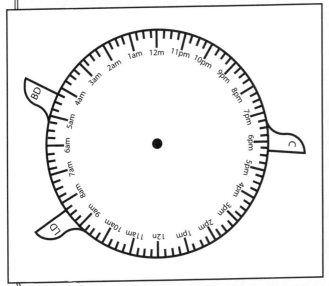

This next part is a bit tricky, but it must be done carefully to make sure your nocturnal can do its job. You're going to draw three "teeth" on this smaller circle; the teeth will have one straight edge and one curved edge, and they will each be labeled with the name of a constellation.

Here we go:

1. Draw the straight edge for the first tooth at exactly 63.4 degrees counterclockwise from midnight—this edge should line up with 4:14 am on the circle. Label this tooth "BD" for the Big Dipper.

2. Draw the straight edge for the second tooth at 124.4 degrees counterclockwise from midnight—this edge should line up with 8:18 am. Label this tooth "LD" for the Little Dipper.

3. Draw the straight edge for the third tooth at 94.7 degrees clockwise from midnight—this edge should line up with 5:41 pm. Label this tooth "C" for Cassiopeia.

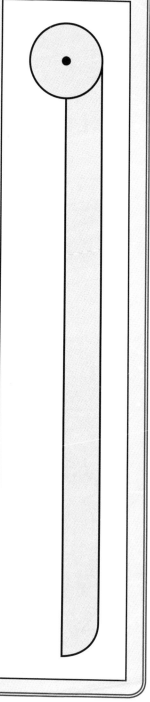

For all three teeth, draw the curved edges as shown. Mark the center of the circle with a dot. Cut out this circle and the teeth, leaving the teeth attached to the circle.

Draw a third circle on the poster board, this one just over 1 inch in diameter (say one-eighth inch over). Mark the center of the circle with a dot, then draw a line from the center of the circle that's at least 9 inches long. (Make sure this line is at least 4 inches longer than the diameter of your largest circle.) Draw another line parallel to this one that connects just at the edge of the circle (see the picture for details). Cut out this circle and its pointer arm.

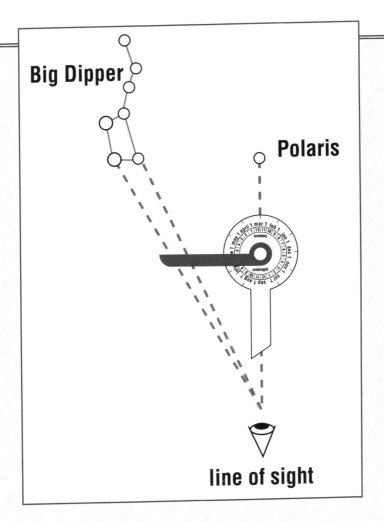

Drill or punch a hole through the center of each of the circles. Make the holes just large enough for the pipe. Place the circles on the pipe, with the smallest circle on top of the middle one, which is on top of the largest one. Screw the nuts onto the pipe. The circles should be loose enough that you can move them, but not so loose that they can move on their own.

To use the nocturnal, first decide whether you want to use the Big Dipper, the Little Dipper, or Cassiopeia. Let's pick the Big Dipper since you used this constellation in chapter two to find Polaris. Set the tooth marked "BD" on the correct date; if the date is May 7, for example, the straight edge of the tooth should line up with the rightmost mark in May.

Hold the nocturnal at arm's length with the handle pointing down. Use the pointer stars on the Big Dipper to find Polaris, then move the nocturnal so that you can see Polaris through the pipe in the center of your nocturnal. While keeping Polaris in sight through the pipe, move the pointer arm until the long edge lines up with the pointer stars in the Big Dipper. The edge of the pointer across the hour sections will show, with an error of about 15 minutes or so, what time it is!

If you want to use the Little Dipper to measure time, set the date with the "LD" tooth on the date, spot Polaris through the nocturnal as usual, and line up the pointer arm with Kochab, the star in the upper right corner of the Little Dipper's cup. To use Cassiopeia as a guide, use the "C" tooth to mark the date and line up the pointer arm with Schedar. Look at the picture if you're not sure where these two stars are located.

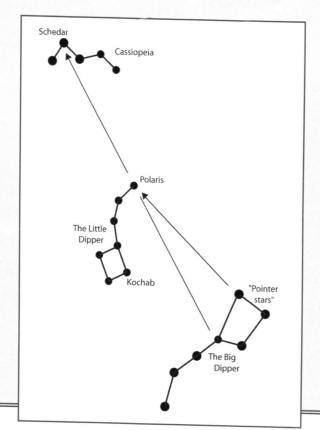

What Is a Clock Anyway?

What's the first thing that comes to mind when you think of a clock? A round surface with arms that point at numbers from 1 to 12? A small box that displays red numbers and flashes 12:00 whenever you lose electricity? These are both *examples* of clocks, but clocks come in all sorts of shapes, sizes, and designs.

In fact, to be a clock, a device requires only two things: a constant or repetitive process that marks off equal pieces of time, and a way to track the pieces and display the results. An Egyptian shadow clock meets both of these requirements. The movement of the shadow across the board marks off the hours of the day, and this same board displays the result of that movement. The klepsydra and sundial work similarly.

Make a candle clock

Tell time with your hands

Create your own incense alarm clock

The Sun is a Clock!??

The sun itself is a "clock" because it moves steadily across the sky, and (if you know what you're doing) you can tell time by measuring its location overhead.

Different cultures have created many types of clocks over the past 10,000 years, and while they didn't work as accurately as today's clocks and watches—even those you get for free in a cereal box—they did a fine job for their time. Here are more examples of timekeeping methods that were good enough:

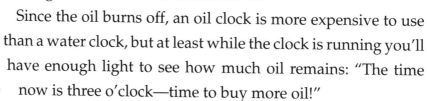

Oil Lamp Just as you can make a water clock by measuring the flow of water, you can make an "oil clock" by measuring the level of oil in a lamp. As the wick burns in an oil lamp, the level of oil remaining drops. You can track time by comparing oil levels against marks on the glass reservoir that holds the oil.

Since the oil burns off, an oil clock is more expensive to use than a water clock, but at least while the clock is running you'll have enough light to see how much oil remains: "The time now is three o'clock—time to buy more oil!"

A modern reproduction of a European oil clock. [courtesy Collectiques.co.uk]

Candles A candle clock is easy to use, but while you won't find one for sale in any department store, it's easy to make your own.

Incense Most people burn incense sticks and cones because they like the smell, but incense can also help you track time. If, for example, an incense stick takes one-and-a-half hours to burn out, then you

SELLING BY THE CANDLE

The seventeenth-century poet John Milton described another way to use candles for timekeeping called "selling by the candle." During an auction, the auctioneer pushed a pin into the side of a burning candle. People could bid for an item until the candle burned down and the pin fell out. When this happened, the bidding stopped and the person with the current high bid got to buy the item.

WORDS TO KNOW

incense: *a slow-burning substance that produces a fragrant odor when burned.*

What two things does a clock have to do to be a clock?

ACTIVITY

Burning the Midnight Wax

You need to choose the right kind of candle to make this clock work. The candle must be the same width from top to bottom, not tapered at the top, and it must be less than 1.5 inches in diameter so that the burning wax falls down the outside of the candle. These are the supplies you'll need for this project:

- candle
- candleholder
- matches
- a marker

Place the candle in a candleholder, then measure the length of the candle that is visible. Light the candle and let it burn for either 30 minutes or an hour.

original candle height

space marks this far apart

Blow out the candle, and once the wax has cooled, measure the candle again to see how much of it has melted away. If, for example, the candle burned three-quarters of an inch in one hour, then make a mark from the top of the candle every three-quarter inches and number the marks. With a supply of these candles you can make a new candle clock any time. If you lose power in your house during a thunderstorm, you can take out a candle clock, light it up, and track how much time passes before power is restored.

Make sure to keep the candle away from open windows and any other drafts because a breeze will make the candle melt faster, burning up time right before your eyes!

can use an incense stick from the same manufacturer to measure this length of time whenever you need to. (As with a candle clock, you need to keep incense away from drafts or else it won't burn at a constant rate.)

Related Story: Short list for fire safety spokeman said to include SpongeBob

The **Times Herald**

Smokey the Bear Resigns
Beloved Icon of Fire Safety
Said to be Upset Over Fire
Being Used to Keep Time

Lorem ipsum dolor sit amet, conse ctetuer adipiscing elit, sed diam no nummy nibh euismod tincidunt ut la oreet dolore magna aliquam erat vo

Lorem ipsum dolor sit amet, conse ctetuer adipiscing elit, sed diam no nummy nibh euismod tincidunt ut la oreet dolore magna aliquam erat vo

The Chinese came up with the idea of using incense for timekeeping, and, as with most creations, many variations on the idea have been used over the years. For example, just as every videotape sold today comes in VHS format, every incense producer made his or her sticks the same length and width as everyone else's so that all sticks burned the same amount of time. After all, once everyone knows that incense burns for an hour, customers won't be happy to buy sticks that last only 50 minutes.

Young boys who served as messengers were not allowed to sleep very much, so they would place a lit incense stick between their toes before they went to sleep. Aren't you glad alarm clocks don't work like this today!

Some Chinese added several perfumes to their incense so that the aroma would change as the stick burned. If you started smelling, say, jasmine, you would know that 30 minutes had passed; once the air filled with a musky smell, you would know it was an hour later.

One example of an even fancier incense alarm clock comes from the nineteenth century. The "clock" is a long piece of wood carved to look like a boat, with a dragon's head at the front. Inside the boat, a piece of pewter holds the incense so that the wood doesn't burn.

A person using this clock places an incense stick flat on the piece of pewter, then lays thin strings over the incense. Each of the strings has a small metal ball tied

What are the different ways that incense worked as a clock?

Dragon incense clock.

to each end. As the incense burns, it also burns through the strings, which causes the metal balls to fall into a bowl placed below the clock. The noise of the metal hitting the bowl sounds like the chime of a modern clock, and as long as the strings are placed evenly across the incense, the clock will be fairly reliable.

Rolling Ball Clock Perhaps you've seen clocks in gift shops that use metal balls to display the hours and minutes. The machine usually has a motorized arm that lifts a ball onto a series of ramps, and the ball rolls until it lands in a space for minutes. When the minutes slot fills up, one falls into a space for hours, and the rest roll to the bottom.

ROLLING BALLS, LAUNCHING ROCKETS

Sir William Congreve (1772–1828) is known to horologists for inventing a unique style of rolling ball clock, but the rest of the world knows him as the inventor

Sir William Congreve the Younger

of the military rocket. The British used his rockets in 1806 against French ships, in 1807 while attacking the city of Copenhagen, and in 1808 during a battle in Spain. Congreve, a lifelong soldier, was present during all of these attacks.

In addition to patenting his method of tracking time with a ball on an inclined plane, Congreve took out patents for paper that could be used to make money that couldn't be forged, a method for protecting buildings against fire, and a way to use rockets to hunt whales!

While fun to watch, these rolling ball clocks aren't very interesting in terms of timekeeping innovation because what keeps the time is the motor that drives the arm, not the metal balls themselves. The metal balls just display the results.

A better example of a rolling ball clock is one William Congreve invented in 1808. The clock consists of a series of interlocking gears and a metal table that tilts back and forth like a seesaw. A metal ball runs down a zigzag path cut into this metal table; after 30 seconds it reaches the end of the path, where it hits a catch that tilts the table in the other direction. The tilting

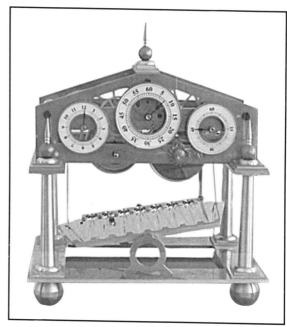

Rolling ball clock designed by William Congreve in 1808.

of the table helps drive the gears of the clock. Hours and minutes are displayed on dials, and the moving ball indicates seconds as it passes under small bridges on the metal table. Calculations show that the metal ball travels more than 12,000 miles in a year!

A clock requires two things:

1. **a constant repetitive process that marks off equal pieces of time.**

2. **a way to track these pieces of time and display the results.**

Hand Sundial Until the eighteenth century most common people could not afford a clock of their own, so they measured time only by the movement of the sun, bells rung in church towers, and sundials on public buildings. However, European peasants in the eighteenth century came up with a cheap way to make a hand sundial with nothing more than their hands and a short stick.

latitude in degrees

ACTIVITY

Make a Hand Sundial

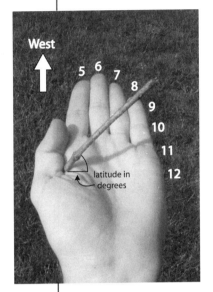

In addition to your hands, you'll also need a stick or pen that's about 6 inches long. If you're measuring time in the morning, hold your left hand, palm up, facing the west (away from the horizon where the sun rose) and place the stick close to the base of your left thumb. The angle formed by the stick and your palm should be roughly equal to your latitude. (Check out the activities in chapter two if you need to find your latitude.)

The shadow of the stick across your hand will give you a general idea of the time, as shown in the pictures.

To measure time after noon, hold the stick at the base of your right thumb and hold your hand, palm up, facing east.

Now, you could use your hands to pick up the telephone and the stick to push buttons to dial the local number that will give you the time, but it's much cooler to read the time of day in the palm of your hand.

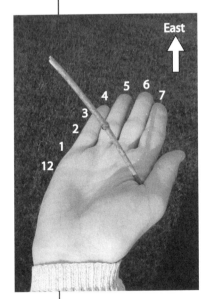

Latitudes for some cities:

New York City	40°34'N	Chicago	41°51'N
San Francisco	37°46'N	Miami	25°46'N
Los Angeles	34°03'N	Houston	29°45'N
Johannesburg, South Africa	26°11'S	Montreal, Canada	46°48'N
Sydney, Australia	33°52'S	Hong Kong	22°18'N

Put time in the palm of your hand! These photos, taken at 10:30 am and 6 pm at a latitude of 42 degrees, show that a stick can do a surprisingly good job of telling time.

ACTIVITY

Make Your Own Incense Clock

Here's a way to tell time and make your house smell good, too. By placing weighted strings at equal distances along a burning incense stick, you can keep track of time as the incense burns.

Be aware: This activity requires the use of incense and matches, so be sure to have your parents' permission before you begin.

For this project you'll need the following materials:

- a foil bread pan
- ruler
- pen
- 12 small metal weights or washers
- watch
- gravel
- 1 stick of incense
- 6 pieces of thread or string
- cookie sheet or other metal tray
- kitchen tongs
- matches

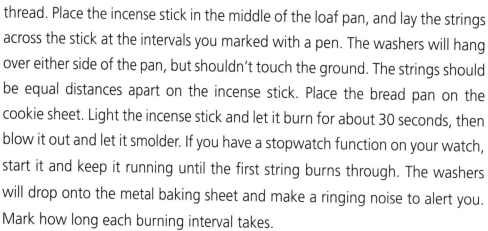

Fill the bread pan almost to the top with gravel. Using a ruler, measure six equal distances along the length of the incense stick. Mark these with a pen. Tie a washer to the end of each piece of thread. Place the incense stick in the middle of the loaf pan, and lay the strings across the stick at the intervals you marked with a pen. The washers will hang over either side of the pan, but shouldn't touch the ground. The strings should be equal distances apart on the incense stick. Place the bread pan on the cookie sheet. Light the incense stick and let it burn for about 30 seconds, then blow it out and let it smolder. If you have a stopwatch function on your watch, start it and keep it running until the first string burns through. The washers will drop onto the metal baking sheet and make a ringing noise to alert you. Mark how long each burning interval takes.

Warning! Be careful when using matches and lighting the incense. Get an adult to help. Never leave the incense unattended. Never touch lit incense. Handle it only with the tongs. When finished, run the stick under water to make sure it is out and will not start a fire.

Escaping the Time Traps of Old

By the year 1000 CE, European and Asian civilizations had several types of time-keeping systems to choose from, but their accuracy ranged from awful to horrible.

Sundials had to be made specially for each latitude and placed precisely facing north—and even then they gave only a rough idea of the time. Hot weather would evaporate water in a klepsydra, and cold would make the water freeze. Candles, oil, incense—all of these gave a general idea of the time, but they were far from precise.

In times past, most people were okay with rough estimates of the time. Children learned from their parents (or worked in the fields!) and didn't have to move from classroom to classroom every 53 minutes. Farmers worked from sunrise to sunset, and they hardly needed a clock to tell them when the sun was up. Knowing the time

Learn why precise timekeeping became important

See how the invention of mechanical clocks began to change society

59

What numeral system changed manufacturing in Europe?

was useful if you could manage it—kind of like doing a split or rolling your tongue into a tube—but hardly necessary.

But that relaxed attitude toward time started changing over the next two centuries. Arabic numerals (0, 1, 2, 3, 4, 5, and so forth) largely replaced Roman numerals (I, II, III, IV, V) in Europe. This mathematics system made adding, subtracting, and multiplying so much easier that manufacturers were able to be more precise and productive.

As manufacturing become more profitable, cities grew richer and built their own armies to fight off the princes and dukes that wanted to control them. As cities grew larger and safer, many Europeans decided to leave the fields and work in factories that made clothing, glassware, and iron tools.

Today we use time clocks and computer log-in systems to track an employee's work hours, but in the factories of the 1200s you had to show up for work "when it was light enough to make out a person's face" at a certain distance. Can you imagine how many arguments this must have caused? Do you have to see just the eyebrows and mouth, or must the nostrils also be visible? What about eye color? A near-sighted person could take off his glasses and get extra sleep since he could argue that it's not light enough for him to see anything!

The Roman Catholic Church, which had a lot of influence throughout Europe at this time, also used general descriptions rather than exact times for when events should occur. For example, instead of saying prayers exactly at 10 am or 6:30 pm, monks would pray "in late morning" or "just before sunset." Monks had to say prayers in a particular order, however, and if they started too late, their schedule would be off for the rest of the day.

Most Europeans still used the system of uneven hours that the Egyptians had invented thousands of years earlier, so work hours and prayer times shifted throughout the year as the length of daylight grew and shrank.

With time always in flux—and work and prayer schedules becoming increasingly difficult to meet due to busier days—Europeans began needing a more accurate timekeeping system. Unknown to them, Asian horologists had already found the basis for something better more than 500 years earlier.

Tales of Tick-Tock

To keep time accurately, you have to be able to divide and measure time in small, regular chunks over and over again. Klepsydras work okay if they're designed so that water flows out at a continuous rate—but at some point the flow of water will end and the timekeeping comes to a halt.

Chinese horologists figured out a way around this problem as far back as 610 CE. A klepsydra in use at that time had a bar on a pivot (much like a teeter-totter) with a container on one end. The container floated in a reservoir of water and was filled slowly through a siphon. When the container was nearly full, a worker would pivot the bar so that the container rose above the reservoir, allowing the water to drain out.

This system allowed someone to check the time continuously by seeing how much water had flowed into or out of the container, but it's not very practical since you need someone on hand to raise or lower the container quite often. If you go on vacation, your clock stops working!

The Chinese solved this problem by making the worker a part of the clock itself. In Su Sung's fabulous water clock of 1090, which you read about back in chapter three, water would flow into a bucket until the weight of the bucket was so heavy that it tripped a lever on the clock. The clock turned until the bucket was past the lever, then the lever would snap back into place to stop the wheel from turning any more and the next bucket would be filled. This process may sound cumbersome, but in fact it took only 24 seconds to fill a bucket and rotate the 30-foot-tall waterwheel, so the clock was a work of genius for that time.

Su Sung's waterclock.

WORDS TO KNOW

siphon: *A tube running from the liquid in a vessel to a lower level outside the vessel so that atmospheric pressure forces the liquid through the tube.*

ESCAPEMENT ESCAPADES

The principle behind escapements is easy: stop something from moving right now so that when it does move again, it will move with more force.

To see this principle in action, imagine Su Sung's water clock without an escapement. Water flows into a bucket, but before the bucket fills up, the wheel starts turning. It turns quickly at first, but then slows a little and finally stops. Maybe a bucket lands right under the water, but maybe not. If not, some water will splash past the bucket, and it will take longer to fill, which means more time will pass before the wheel turns again.

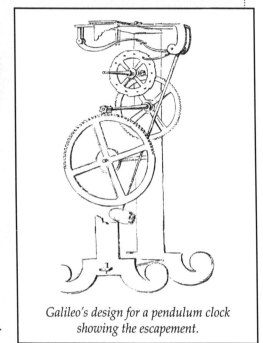

Galileo's design for a pendulum clock showing the escapement.

Clocks rely on movement that is regularly timed and evenly measured; escapements make this possible. Manufacturers work in the same way on their production lines. If you make ketchup, you must set up your machines so that an exact amount of ketchup squirts into each bottle before the bottle is capped. Machines must then place the same number of bottles in each box before closing and sealing the box. If you didn't do this, customers and supermarkets would stop buying from you. Similarly, if a clock's escapement didn't work properly, you wouldn't buy the "time" the clock was trying to sell you!

The lever on Su Sung's clock is an example of an escapement, a device that regulates short periods of time so that they're always the same length. As long as the water kept flowing, Su Sung's clock would rotate exactly ten degrees every 24 seconds, turning the main shaft of the waterwheel and driving other gears that moved the time-telling displays on the rest of the clock.

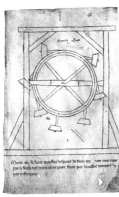

Courtesy Ross Woodrow & The University of Newcastle.

One of Honnecourt's designs for a perpetual motion machine.

The movement of the escapement is what creates the familiar tick-tock sound that people associate with old-fashioned clocks. Without that regular beat, the clock won't be tracking equal intervals of time and will be useless to anyone looking at it.

European Escape

Although the Chinese had hundreds of years of experience with the escapement, the idea seems to have arrived in Europe from a different source: French architect Villard de Honnecourt.

Honnecourt designed cathedrals for a living, but like many educated people in the Middle Ages, he had other interests as well. His sketchbooks include such ideas as a hand warmer for bishops to use during high mass and the first European attempt at a perpetual motion machine.

Honnecourt's vision of perpetual motion was doomed to failure, but his research led him to sketch out the first clock escapements seen in Europe. The sketch, titled "How to make an angel point with his finger towards the sun,"

PERPETUAL MOTION

The idea behind perpetual motion is that if you create a machine that gives off more energy than it consumes, you can make the machine run forever. Unfortunately, scientists researched perpetual motion for hundreds of years before they finally discovered that it couldn't be done. Just as you must eat meals regularly if you want to run around and play all day, machines must have a steady supply of energy coming in because they all lose energy in the form of heat or friction while they work.

WORDS TO KNOW

escapement: *a device that regulates short periods of time so they are always the same length.*
perpetual motion machine: *a machine that can continue to do work indefinitely without drawing energy from an external force.*

described how to use a wheel with spokes, several axles, a weight, and a rope to rotate the figure of an angel on the roof of a church. The rope is wound around the angel's ankles and attached to the weight. The weight turns the wheel axle until the rope hits a spoke on the wheel; the weighted rope stops moving briefly as it bounces off the spoke, then it falls again until it hits another spoke. As the rope moves, it slowly turns the angel at a rate that should match the movement of the sun.

DID HE OR DIDN'T HE?

Based on a look at Villard de Honnecourt's sketchbooks, he seems to have been everywhere and done everything. He built cathedrals, directed the digging of underground passageways, designed an automatic sawmill, and much more.

But look closer at de Honnecourt's history, and it's not clear what he actually did. He left no records in guild registers, contract files, tax payments, or other paper documents that medieval builders normally left behind. His name remains on no building. He was born sometime around the 1220s or 1230s, but no one knows for sure.

All we have to go on are the sketches that de Honnecourt left behind. Do they show original drawings of his creations, or did he copy existing buildings and machines and claim them as his own designs? Nearly eight hundred years after he lived, how can we prove or disprove what he said he did? No one knows for sure.

Pages from the sketchbooks of de Honnecourt

WORDS TO KNOW

verge escapement: *clock escapement that uses vertical rods with paddles.*

foliot: *a lever with weighted arms attached to the paddled rod of the verge escapement.*

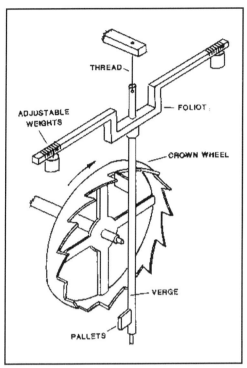

Although Honnecourt never built this clock—and it's not clear whether his design would have worked in real life—mechanical clocks using a similar design did start appearing in the late thirteenth and early fourteenth centuries.

Instead of a rope, though, the verge escapement uses a vertical metal rod with two paddles on it. As the spoked wheel turns, a spoke hits one paddle and turns the rod to knock the paddle out of the way. However, as the rod turns, the other paddle hits the spoked wheel; the wheel knocks this paddle out of the way, which turns the rod in the other direction and makes the first paddle hit the wheel again. The spoked wheel wants to spin fast because of the weight on it, but the paddles let it turn only one spoke at a time. Tick-tock-tick-tock . . .

The speed at which the wheel turns is determined by the foliot, a lever with weights on the end of each arm that's attached to the paddled rod. By moving the weights on the arms, you can make the escapement move faster or slower. You've probably noticed a similar effect on a teeter-totter. If you sit close to the end of the teeter-totter, you can lift more weight than if you sit near the middle. Similarly, if the weight is moved to the end of the foliot, the escapement will move more slowly because it's harder to move the weight.

Look, Ma, No Hands!

Europeans already had plenty of experience with gears from their knowledge of windmills and watermills. These devices used the power of wind and water to turn gears, which then turned other gears, which moved heavy millstones to grind grain. By arranging the gears the right way, mill operators could increase the power provided by wind and water to move millstones that weighed several tons.

If you've ridden a bicycle with multiple gears, you already know how gears work. When you ride up a hill, for example, you switch down in gears so that the chain is on a large gear by the pedals and a small gear by the back wheel. Doing this lets you put more energy into the small gear and turn the back wheel more easily. When you ride down a hill, however, you move the chain onto a small gear by the pedals and a large gear by the back wheel. Now you have to pedal only a little bit to turn the back wheel a lot. Using these same ideas, the first clockmakers placed gears with verge escapements to transfer the small back-and-forth motion of the paddled rod into more power.

What did they do with all this power? Take over the world? No, they automated clock functions that people used to do by hand. For hundreds of years, monks had monitored klepsydra or candle clocks or hourglasses and rung bells to mark

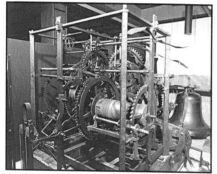

the hours and the times for prayer. Thanks to the regular ticking of the escapement and the use of many gears, clocks could now automatically ring bells each hour.

In fact, ringing bells was the *only* thing the first mechanical clocks did. They had no faces or moving arms; only gears and levers made to strike a bell. The word clock, which didn't appear until the fourteenth century, even comes from the old

Early mechanical clock showing a bell.

French word *cloque*, which means bell.

What's more, these clocks struck a bell only once each hour, no matter what time of day it was. At ten o'clock, it rang once; at eleven o'clock, it rang once; and so on. This meant people who heard the bell still had to look to the sky to get an idea of what time it was. Striking a bell a number of times equal to the hour seems to have been

> ...ringing bells was the *only* thing the first mechanical clocks did.

developed around the mid-1300s, when clockmakers figured out how to use a separate set of gears to count off the hours.

The hour hand was another early improvement on the clock, but in the earliest designs the hour hand didn't move; instead the face labeled with the hours was just another gear that turned as time passed.

Just as Su Sung and other horologists had included moving astronomical displays in their klepsydra, the builders of the first mechanical clocks soon added many moving parts to their creations. The Italian Giovanni de Dondi, for example, spent 16 years in the middle of the fourteenth century building a 24-hour clock that included the movement of the planets and the moon. The clock in the Wells Cathedral, built around 1392, had figures of knights that jousted every hour.

An engraving of the Wells Cathedral Clock, originally built in 1392.

Nearly all of the mechanical clocks built in the 1300s were used in churches, cathedrals, and government buildings. In addition to being expensive to build, the weighted rope that moved the escapement was really long and needed to drop a long distance, so church steeples and towers at city hall were almost the only buildings tall enough. What's more, the clocks were huge and heavy. The clock at Wells Cathedral, for example, was four feet high. Try fitting that on your nightstand!

But Are They Better?

The mechanical clocks of fourteenth-century Europe were an improvement over the sundials and klepsydras that most people used. The clocks worked day and night, summer and winter, and they didn't need a translator to watch the water flow and then ring a bell to let everyone else know an hour had passed. Once hour hands appeared, people could look at the church tower to know the time instead of counting how many bells had passed.

Where does the word clock come from?

Why were mechanical clocks of the 1300s mainly used in churches, cathedrals, and government buildings?

With the introduction of escapements and the tick-tock of time, the idea that hours should be longer in the summer and shorter in the winter faded away. Yes, people could move the weights on the foliot to adjust how quickly time passed, but it was easier to adjust to the idea that hours should be the same length throughout the year. People came to realize that night and day weren't two different things that had to be counted separately, but rather that night and day were connected and one flowed easily into the other.

Recoil escapement.

Having clocks visible on churches and city halls also got rid of the messy way that employees and employers tracked work hours. Instead of starting work "when it was light enough to make out a person's face," people started and stopped work at particular times. If workers were late, they were paid less; if they worked more hours, they earned more.

Despite all these improvements, the mechanical clocks weren't any more accurate than klepsydras or other time-tracking systems. They lost or gained up to 15 minutes a day, and people would have to reset them by looking at sundials.

The idea for the escapement was wonderful, but in real life, early clockmakers couldn't make the gears so that they worked smoothly. The teeth on the gears stuck together or were too loose. People used oil to make the gears turn better, but the oil would collect dirt and dust that slowed the machine. The oil would also thicken or get thin as the temperature changed, which affected the clock's gears. Churches no longer needed someone to ring the bell every hour, but they still needed someone to oil the gears and reset the hour hand once a day.

Still, the escapement was a break with the past. Mechanical clocks were a new design that already matched the accuracy of candle clocks, klepsydra, hourglasses, and other time-telling devices of old. They would only get better in the years ahead.

How accurate were the first mechanical clocks?

BACK AND FORTH AND BACK AND FORTH

When last we checked the history of the clock, the year was 1400 and mechanical clocks had provided a breakthrough experience for Europeans. Methods of telling time were available on the outside towers of most churches and government buildings, and the general population was becoming more aware of the value of time in terms of work and leisure.

By 1500, the time-telling situation in Europe was—well, pretty much the same. Few people in Europe could afford to buy mechanical clocks, so they used sandglasses in their homes instead. Real accuracy in timekeeping was still a goal, rather than reality.

One area that clock designers had improved upon was the size of the clock, with "improvement" in this case meaning "shrunk to as small a size as possible." Clockmakers wanted to be able to sell their goods to everyone, after

Recreate Galileo's pendulum experiment

Meet the clockmaker that solved the "longitude problem"

Figure out your longitude

all, and the only way to do this was to shrink the clocks and make them cost less.

Unfortunately for clockmakers, iron in the 1400s was filled with impurities, so it was difficult to shape metal to the small sizes needed. Make a small sizing error on a 3-foot-wide gear wheel, and the gear wheel will likely still do its thing as it grinds and spins; make the same error on a gear wheel only 6 inches wide, and you're likely to be starting over from scratch.

As the decades passed though, clockmakers became more skilled at creating smaller clocks that could be carried while traveling, and by 1500, wealthy Europeans were buying small clocks in a frenzy, clocks that were often encrusted with jewels and gold. Queen Elizabeth I even owned a small ring watch that could scratch its owner's fingers like an alarm at particular times of day.

The smaller clocks, however, were designed very much like the earliest mechanical clocks, meaning they used a long, weighted cord to move the foliot and verge escapement that regulated the gears. In many situations—such as sailing the sea or riding in a bouncy coach—a weight-driven clock was next to worthless, and sailors and riders had to go back to staring at the sun or breaking out the sextant.

Queen Elizabeth I

Springing a New Time Solution

Between 1500 and 1510, Peter Henlein, a locksmith from the German town of Nuremberg, discovered how to drive the gears of a clock with springs. Yes, springs! Today, when we think about springs, we tend to think of box-spring mattresses and pogo sticks, but springs come in many shapes other than a wound-up coil that looks like a spiced

Peter Henlein

Artist Rendering

The *Times Herald*

Timepieces Getting Smaller and Smaller
Clocks worn as jewelry. . . the future of timekeeping?

Lorem ipsum dolor sit amet, conse ctetuer adipiscing elit, sed diam no nummy nibh euismod tincidunt ut la oreet dolore magna aliquam erat vo lutpat. Ut wisi enim ad minim venia m, quis nostrud exerci tation ullamc orper suscipit lobortis nisl ut aliquip ex ea commodo consequat. Duis

Lorem ipsum dolor sit amet, conse ctetuer adipiscing elit, sed diam no nummy nibh euismod tincidunt ut la oreet dolore magna aliquam erat vo lutpat. Ut wisi enim ad minim venia m, quis nostrud exerci tation ullamc orper suscipit lobortis nisl ut aliquip ex ea commodo consequat. Duis

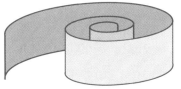

curly fry. The springs that Henlein used resemble a long, thin piece of stiff metal that's rolled up in a spiral, kind of like a cinnamon bun but with less flavor.

In a "Nuremberg Egg," to use Henlein's name for his spring-driven creation, the mainspring would slowly unwind and drive the gears. By replacing the heavy weights that drove the escapement that moved the gears, the mainspring made it possible for clockmakers to create smaller clocks and watches—even portable ones. The springs weren't perfect; as they unwound, the gears of the clock slowed, and if the spring unwound completely, the clock stopped. To keep a spring-driven clock running properly, the owner of the clock had to wind up the spring several times a day.

Henlein's Nuremberg Egg.

To solve the problem of the mainspring's uneven power, Jacob Zech of Prague invented the fusee, or spiral

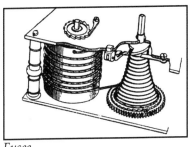

Fusee.

pulley, around 1525 to smooth out the power of the mainspring. The fusee is a cone-shaped, grooved pulley that turns slower when the spring has lots of power and faster when the spring is winding down. The design of the fusee evened out the mainspring's power, but these spring-driven clocks and watches still weren't very accurate.

As the 1500s drew to a close, owning personal timepieces and having clocks throughout the home were considered status symbols, and even members of the middle class—merchants, bankers, and lawyers—could afford their own clock or watch. But that doesn't mean the clocks were highly accurate: the very best clocks were off by only one minute a day, but it was much more likely that a clock would gain or lose up to 15 minutes every day.

WORDS TO KNOW

fusee: *a spiral pulley used to even out the power of a mainspring in a watch.*

How much time would the average clock of the late 1500s gain or lose every day?

Swinging for the Fences

Nearly all of the improvements to clock design from the years 1300 to 1600 amounted to little more than tinkering with the headlights in a car with only three wheels. Yes, clockmakers were using better materials and making smaller and smaller gears to fit into pocket watches and other devices, but the basic design hadn't changed over that 300-year period: A falling weighted rope, which was repeatedly stopped and released by a verge escapement, turned a bunch of gears that turned an arm around a dial or rang bells. The design worked, but it seemed to be as good as it would get.

However, you never know what tricks science is going to pull out of its bag. Just when you think you understand the world around you, scientists will often find out something else about the world and give you something brand new to think about.

RENAISSANCE MAN, PART I

When Galileo Galilei was young, his father Vincenzo wanted him to be a doctor. Galileo, who was born in 1564, agreed to the idea—then went to the University of Pisa and instead studied mathematics and natural philosphy. Eventually, Vincenzo learned of his son's deception, but Galileo's teachers convinced Vincenzo that his son was a natural at math.

Soon Galileo was teaching math courses at universities, and he also taught astronomy and researched the theory of motion, that is, how objects fall and move through space. One of Galileo's most famous findings is that objects fall at the same rate of speed. Supposedly Galileo proved this by dropping two balls of different weights from the Leaning Tower of Pisa, but this story is most likely untrue.

In 1609, Galileo heard about a remarkable spyglass that let a person see

In the 1630s, the Italian inventor and astronomer Galileo Galilei noticed that lamps hanging on chains from the ceiling of his church took the same amount of time to swing back and forth no matter how far the lamp moved. This puzzled Galileo because common sense would suggest that if one lamp swings five feet in an arc and another lamp swings 15 feet, the lamp that swings 15 feet should take three times as long because it covers three times as much area.

Equal time elapses in both scenarios

Galileo tested his observation many times, and much to his surprise he discovered that swinging objects can cover different distances in the same amount of time.

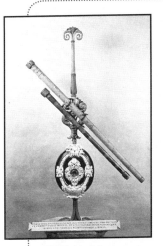

Galileo's telescope.

distant objects as if they were close. He quickly built his own telescope, and within a year he made many fantastic discoveries: he saw mountains on the moon, found out that the Milky Way was made up of stars, spotted four moons around Jupiter, and noted that Venus had phases like earth's moon. These findings all were evidence that earth wasn't at the center of the universe, as many religious people believed, but rather that the earth and all the other planets revolved about the sun, as astronomer Nicolas Copernicus argued nearly a century earlier.

Galileo kept quiet about his opinions until 1632, when he wrote a book that explained why Copernicus was right about the structure of the solar system. He was soon punished by the Pope and put under house arrest, but this didn't break his spirit. As Galileo put it, "In questions of science, the authority of a thousand is not worth the humble reasoning of a single individual."

Galileo died in 1642, and in 1992, 350 years after his death, the Catholic Church finally admitted that it had made errors in its case against Galileo.

What did Galileo discover while observing lamps suspended on a chain swinging back and forth?

ACTIVITY

Putting Pendulum Power to the Test

Much has changed since the time of Galileo, but thankfully the forces of physics remain the same. This means you can recreate Galileo's experiments with pendulums to find out for yourself how they work. For this activity, you'll need:

- **4 rulers**
- **masking tape**
- **12 washers at least as large as a nickel**
- **three 20-inch-long pieces of string**
- **a timer**

You'll use one ruler for measuring and the other three to create supports for your pendulums. Tape three of the rulers to one or more desks that are the same height. Tie one washer to one piece of string, then do it again. Tape the loose ends of these two pieces of string to two different rulers, measuring the string so that each is exactly 10 inches long. You have created two identical pendulums.

To test Galileo's finding, pull one washer back two inches and another washer back six inches. Release them at the same time, and pay attention to when the strings are straight up and down. The strings should be vertical at the same time, even though one washer travels much farther than another.

To carry out other tests like Galileo, play around with the variables in your activity—the length of string and the amount of weight on the string—to see what causes a pendulum to swing faster or slower. How many washers do you need to add to make a pendulum that swings twice as fast? How short must you make the string to achieve the same result? Can you add more weight and lengthen the string to create a pendulum that swings at the same rate as your original one?

The key discovery was that the lamps (or any weight on a rope or chain) don't just swing on the rope; they actually fall first, and the rope kind of catches them and pulls them along. When the lamp falls, it picks up speed, so it swings faster than a lamp that doesn't fall as far. The faster speed of the one lamp makes up for the longer distance, so the travel time for both lamps will be the same.

Wait a second: an object that moves at a constant rate? Sounds like the start of a clock.

same distance traveled, shorter time for scenario B

Further tests led Galileo to discover that what matters most to the speed of the swinging object is the length of the rope or cord holding it: the longer the rope, the longer the amount of time the object will take to complete an entire arc. By adjusting the length of the cord, an object could be made to swing at exactly the rate needed to move the gears of a clock. Galileo sketched out the design for a pendulum clock in 1637, but he never had a chance to build it.

In 1656, unaware of Galileo's findings and design, the Dutch scientist Christian Huygens built a pendulum clock of his own, using the pendulum to time the movement of the escapement. If left alone, the pendulum would eventually slow down and stop moving, but Huygens designed the clock so that the movement of the escapement gave the pendulum a little push with each swing.

Huygens had a great idea, but the pendulum didn't work quite right with the verge escapement. Although Huygens tried to fix the problem on his own, the solution actually came from another scientist about 15 years later. The anchor escapement, named after its shape, swings back and forth in much less space

WORDS TO KNOW

pendulum clock: *a clock using a swinging pendulum to move its gears.*

anchor escapement: *an escapement shaped like an anchor that made pendulum clocks much more accurate.*

than the verge escapement, and the shorter distance makes the pendulum more accurate. Success!

Riding the Waves

Success, unfortunately, is not always permanent. While Huygens' pendulum clock did work well on land, the pendulum worked no better on ships than clocks

---

RENAISSANCE MAN, PART II

Like Galileo, Christian Huygens (1629–1695), was a man who studied nearly everything. While being tutored at home, for example, Huygens learned geometry, built mechanical models, and played the lute. While at the University of Leiden, he studied both law and mathematics.

Later in his life, Huygens served on a team of diplomats and learned how to build telescopes and grind his own lenses. His astronomical work led him to discover the rings of Saturn and Saturn's moon, Titan. Astronomy requires

accurate timekeeping, and that's what pushed Huygens to develop the pendulum clock.

Huygens designed but never built an internal combustion engine that used gunpowder for fuel. He also showed that objects that collide neither gain nor lose momentum, which fixed an error in the work of his friend, René Descartes.

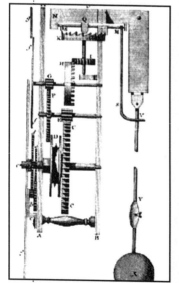

Huygens' pendulum clock.

Near the end of his life, Huygens wrote "Cosmotheoros," an essay about the possibility of life on other worlds, and an essay on light in which he explained the laws of reflection and refraction. Of his own work, Huygens said, "Great difficulties are felt at first and these cannot be overcome except by starting from experiments."

How many miles wide is each degree of longitude at the equator?

Lines of Longitude

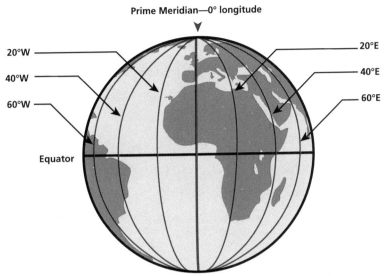

In any path around the earth from east to west, there are 360 degrees of longitude, just as any circle has 360 degrees—but the width of each degree of longitude will depend on where the path lies. If you're close to the North Pole, each degree is much shorter than it is near the equator.

made with verge escapements—and without accurate clocks, ship captains had trouble determining their longitude at sea.

While latitude measures how far a location is north or south of the equator, longitude measures how far a location is east or west of a fixed point. This fixed starting point is called the prime meridian and is located in Greenwich, England. Like latitude, longitude is measured in degrees, and 360 degrees of longitude make one complete trip around the earth.

Since the earth is about 24,900 miles around at the equator, each degree of longitude is at most 70 miles wide. (24,900 divided by 360 equals 69.16.) Near the North or South Pole, however, a degree of longitude might be only 10 miles wide!

More importantly for sailors, if you travel 15 degrees of longitude to the east, local time moves ahead by one hour (360 degrees divided by 24 hours equals

WORDS TO KNOW

longitude: *a measurement of how far a location is east or west of the prime meridian.*
prime meridian: *0 degrees longitude, in Greenwich, England.*

15 degrees per hour). Traveling 15 degrees west moves local time back by one hour. If you know the local times at two points—and definitely know the location of one point—you can then find out where you are.

To understand how this works, imagine that you ride for an hour in a car without a mileage indicator, but you really need to know how many miles you drove. How will you do it?

Well, first look at what you do know: you know what time you left the starting point and the current time; you know the speed that you drove at because you threw a log out the window, actually um, you looked at the speedometer; you know your starting point because you left from your driveway.

With all this information, you can figure out how many miles you are from the starting point because you know how long you drove at what speed. If you also looked at a compass while you rode, you'd even know your exact current location!

English sailors knew how to find their latitude, track their speed, and find the local time, but they needed to know the time in a fixed location—and this is where it all went wrong. They tried to keep a clock on board that was set to local time in Greenwich, but conditions at sea and changes in temperature made the clocks less accurate, which put sailors in constant danger. If they didn't know their location they couldn't navigate accurately. In 1707, for example, four ships crashed on England's Isles of Scilly, killing more than 2,000 sailors.

For an island nation like England, this situation had to end. England was starting to build an empire of colonies around the world, but without good navigation skills, their navy would be much less effective.

Map of Britain, 1616.

To encourage scientists to solve the longitude problem, in 1714 the British Parliament offered 20,000 pounds (equal to many millions of dollars today) to anyone who could provide a chronometer clock that was accurate enough to tell sailors where they were on the ocean within a half-degree of longitude.

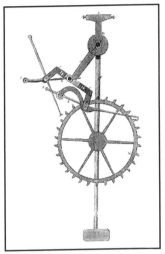

Grasshopper escapement mechanism invented by Harrison.

With that much money being offered, the Board of Longitude was flooded with proposed solutions, none of which proved to be good enough. In fact, the solution to the longitude problem didn't come for decades. The man who found the solution was John Harrison, who designed his first clock in 1715 at the age of 23.

Over his lifetime, Harrison, a brilliant Englishman who taught himself science and clockmaking, built many fabulous timekeeping devices including a clock made entirely of wood (which is still running to this day) and an entirely new escapement called the grasshopper escapement. Harrison's clocks were so accurate that the best of them were off by at most one second per month.

In 1730, after many years of work on different clock designs, Harrison visited London and met with Edmund Halley, discoverer of Halley's Comet, and George Graham, the country's leading clockmaker. Graham was highly impressed by Harrison and lent him money so that Harrison could spend the next five years working on what was known as Harrison-1, or H-1. The clock wasn't tested until a year later when Harrison and H-1 sailed round trip to Lisbon, Portugal. On the way home, Harrison's clock let the captain know that he was more than 60 miles west of where he thought he was!

Courtesy National Maritime Museum, London

John Harrison's first chronometer, H1.

WORDS TO KNOW

chronometer: *a very accurate timepiece used in navigation to determine longitude.*

grasshopper escapement: *an escapement developed by John Harrison that made clocks more accurate.*

Instead of resting on his laurels, Harrison immediately went back to the Board of Longitude and asked for additional funds to make a clock as good as H-1 but smaller. Harrison-2 withstood extreme temperatures and violent shaking, but it turned out to be heavier than H-1, so Harrison started work on H-3.

Harrison worked on H-3 for the next 20 years, trying to fix small problems he found in H-1 and H-2. Eventually, though, he realized that H-3 was never going to work, so he put it aside and started work on something new. Within two years, Harrison completed H-4, which turned out to be only five inches in diameter, one of the smallest navigation clocks ever.

When H-4 was finally tested on an 81-day trip to Jamaica in 1761, the clock lost a total of five seconds on the trip. Harrison was clearly the most skilled clockmaker in England and possibly the world, yet he had to wait another 11 years before being paid by King George III.

Why the long wait for payday? British scientists on the Board of Longitude argued that Harrison got lucky with H-4 because there was no way a clock—especially one that small—could be that accurate. Other scientists in the Royal Society of London hoped to win the prize themselves, so they argued for their solutions to the longitude problem over Harrison's H-4.

To prove that H-4 worked, Harrison had to hand over details on the clock, create another from scratch, and let another clockmaker use his design to create yet another copy. Harrison recommended Larcum Kendall, and Kendall's K-1 was later used by Captain Cook during a three-year voyage from the tropics to the Antarctic. K-1 was never off by more than eight seconds during the entire trip, prompting Cook to call the watch "our faithful guide through all the vicissitudes of climates." King George himself tested Harrison's clock in 1772, and by the following year, Harrison was finally awarded the prize money and recognized as the one who solved the longitude problem.

Map of Captain Cook's voyages.

ACTIVITY

Looking for Longitude

You learned how to use a quadrant to determine your latitude in chapter two; now it's time to figure out your longitude, how far you are east or west of the prime meridian, the line marking 0 degrees longitude in Greenwich, England.

You need:

• 2 clocks

• paper and pencil

First, you need to find out what time it is in Greenwich, England. Visit **www.Greenwichmeantime.com** for the exact time in Greenwich to the second. Set one clock to this time.

Next, at midday wherever you are, set the other clock to noon when the sun is directly overhead. To find out when noon happens locally—and not just noon in your time zone—use a sundial and wait until the shadow of the gnomon is directly in line with the gnomon itself. Now compare the two clocks—by how much time do they differ? The earth rotates about 15 degrees per hour, so if the clocks differ by, for instance, exactly six hours,

Eastern Hemisphere

Western Hemisphere

How did John Harrison's clocks get their names?

What famous explorer used the K-1 chronometer?

then you are either 90 degrees west or 90 degrees (15 degrees multiplied by 6 equals 90 degrees) east of Greenwich. If the clocks differ by, say, 6 hours and 20 minutes, then you multiply 15 degrees by 6.33 hours (20 minutes is one-third or 0.33 of an hour).

How do you know whether you are east or west of Greenwich? Easy—if you live in North or South America or in areas nearby, you live in the Western Hemisphere and are west of Greenwich. If you don't, then you are east of Greenwich.

Here are a few longitudes for places you've probably heard of:

Honolulu, Hawaii: 157° West

San Francisco: 122° West

Disneyland, California: 117° West

Galapagos Islands: 90° West

New York City: 73° West

Machu Picchu, Peru: 72° West

Paris, France: 2° East

Cairo, Egypt, home of the pyramids: 31° East

Moscow: 37° East

Sydney, Australia: 151° East

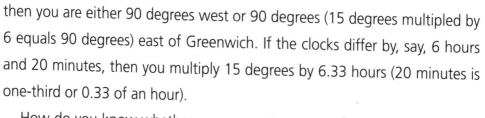

San Francisco, CA—122° west

Machu Picchu, Peru—72° west

Prime Meridian—0°

Paris, France—2° east

Cairo, Egypt—31° east

Honolulu, HI—157° west

International Date Line—180°

Sydney, Australia—151° east

WORDS TO KNOW

International Date Line: *an imaginary line that zigs and zags through the Pacific Ocean (to avoid going through any land) that is at 180 degrees longitude. One the west side of the line it is one day later than on the east side. It is where 180 degrees west meets 180 degrees east.*

ANY WAY YOU SLICE IT . . .

Throughout mankind's efforts to create accurate timekeeping devices, one fact about time has often been ignored: In general, units of time are completely arbitrary. Weeks, hours, seconds—we created them to help us organize our lives, but there's nothing real about them, nothing physical that we can track down, point at, and say, "Look, Ma! That's the third second we've spotted on this trip!"

People have even argued about what a day is, because a day can be measured at least two different ways. One way is to measure how much distance passes between noon and noon; this solar day is the one used most often. Another way is to look at the sidereal day, which is measured by how long it takes the earth to rotate once on its axis.

See the difference between a solar and sidereal day

Connect longitude to the concept of time zones

See why time zones are still changing today

WORDS TO KNOW

solar day: *how much time passes between noon and noon.*

sidereal day: *how long it takes the earth to rotate once on its axis.*

83

ACTIVITY

What a Difference a Day Makes

To see how the solar and sidereal days differ, ask your parents for a quarter and a penny. Place the coins flat up on a table so that George (the sun) and Abe (the earth) stare at one another. Turn Abe counterclockwise one complete turn so that he faces the same direction; this equals one rotation of the earth on its axis. To include the earth's movement around the sun, move Abe a bit counterclockwise around George without rotating Abe any further.

Since Abe faces the same direction, he sees the same background he did to begin with. This counts as a sidereal day as it's the same as one complete rotation of the earth bringing the same stars directly overhead. But Abe no longer looks directly at George; to stare at the Founding Father, Abe must rotate just a tiny bit more counterclockwise. This extra bit of rotation (nearly 4 minutes worth in the case of earth) completes one solar day.

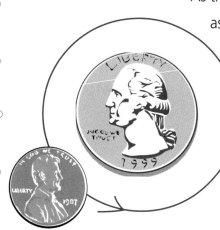

As this experiment makes clear, even something as a simple as a day can't be defined on its own. You must describe the relationship between objects and their movement to explain exactly how long a day lasts. It's a tricky idea, but one we hope you now understand, therefore making you richer in knowledge—and richer by 26 cents as well!

The word "sidereal" comes from the Latin word for "star." Using sidereal days, a location on earth would have the same stars and constellations overhead at the same time each day.

These days might seem to be equal at first, but the sidereal day is shorter than the solar day by 3 minutes and 56 seconds because the earth revolves around the sun at the same time it rotates on its axis. Because of this, the sun moves in relation to the billions of other stars in the sky, and that's why the two days differ.

An Hour in the Hand Is Worth 50 Minutes in the Bush

Even though an hour is a made-up period of time, most everyone agrees how long an hour lasts. The problem in the 1800s, though, was that not everyone agreed on when the hour *started*.

Pendulum clocks lost less than a minute per day, so accuracy of the clocks wasn't a big deal. The problem was that most people set their clocks at noon, either by the sun overhead or by church bells—and noon happened at a different time in almost every town. After all, the sun is directly overhead in Boston before it's overhead in New York, which is before it's overhead in Pittsburgh, and so on. In fact, it's noon somewhere in the United States for more than three hours—and that's not even counting Alaska and Hawaii!

Unlike the four large time zones we use today, the United States of 1860 actually had around 300 different time zones. Every large city set its own time based on when the sun was overhead, so when the clock read noon in Chicago, it was 12:24 in Cleveland; 12:13 in Cincinnati; 12:09 in Louisville, Kentucky; 11:50 in St. Louis; and 11:48 in Dubuque, Iowa.

In the early 1800s, when families traveled by stagecoach and wagons, having different times in different cities wasn't a big problem. After all, traveling from New York to Boston would take an entire day, so what did it matter if you lost 15 minutes on the way? When you arrived in town, you could just look for the nearest church tower and reset your watch.

However, the hundreds of local times did cause trouble once the railroads became more popular and allowed people to travel long distances quickly. If a train travels from Atlanta to Birmingham to New Orleans, for example, which times should be listed on the train schedule? The local times in each city? If so, then you need a separate clock on the train to track each of those times. But how long does the actual train ride take? That would require yet another clock. You'd need a giant pocket to hold all those pocket watches!

WATCHING THE STARS, COUNTING THE HOURS

King Charles II founded the Royal Greenwich Observatory at Greenwich in London in 1675. What did he hope to achieve by having astronomers scan the heavens? He wanted British ships to sail safely throughout the world.

This may seem an odd concept, but as we explained in chapter 6, you can find out your longitude—that is, your position east-to-west—by knowing your current time and the time at another location. Sailors started getting lost in large numbers in the late 1400s, hundreds of years before John Harrison created H-4, when they sailed out of the Mediterranean Sea and began exploring the oceans while creating national empires. Christopher Columbus, for example, thought he had reached the Indian Ocean because he couldn't track longitude and had no idea of the world's actual size.

Slowly sailors realized the true size of the world, but no one was able to figure out a practical solution. Around 1600, Spain and Holland offered huge rewards to anyone who could solve the longitude problem. Within a decade, Galileo offered

The north facade of the Royal Greenwich Observatory in the late seventeenth century.

? WORDS TO KNOW

railway time: *a standard time used by railroads that stayed the same, regardless of location.*

telegraph: *a communication system that transmits electric impulses, usually in Morse code.*

Steam locomotive.

Rather than track the time in each city they visited, railway companies from the 1830s on decided to keep railway time, which would be the same across the entire country. (Samuel Morse developed the telegraph around this time, and this new communication tool helped railway companies synchronize their clocks from coast to coast.) Having only one time made it easier for the railroads, but anyone who wanted to travel by train still had to figure out what railway time equaled in local time.

a solution based on his recent discovery of Jupiter's four moons. The moons regularly crossed into Jupiter's shadow and disappeared from view, and Galileo tracked these movements so that anyone could determine what time it is in Europe by viewing these moons.

This solution would have worked if anyone could use telescopes on moving ships and keep watch of the moons until they saw exactly when a moon traveled into Jupiter's shadow. While Galileo's plan failed, a similar solution was proposed where a sailor could use the position of earth's moon among the stars to determine time in England.

Charles II liked the idea, but was shocked to find out that the country's astronomers didn't know enough about the movement of these heavenly bodies. He named Rev. John Flamsteed the first Astronomer Royal and ordered him to set up an observatory from which the moon's and stars' movement could be tracked.

Flamsteed held this position for 44 years, and over the decades the Royal Greenwich Observatory came to symbolize time in England and, thanks to sea charts sold to sailors from other countries, throughout the world. Even today, the Observatory's first mission is to track the sun, moon, and planets and create accurate star catalogs.

Britain, and most other nations, suffered from the same wrinkles in time as the United States, but in 1847 the British government solved the problem by passing a law that required all railroads to use Greenwich mean time (GMT), the time kept by the Greenwich Observatory. Within eight years, 98 percent of all public clocks in Great Britain were set to GMT.

Officials in the United States weren't as organized as their British counterparts, primarily because America is a lot larger than Britain. Having only one time across the land would have had Californians eating breakfast at 10 am, getting to work at noon, and taking a lunch break at 3 pm when everyone in New York would already be thinking about their evening meal!

In 1870, Professor Charles Dowd proposed a new system that would

divide the United States into four vertical time zones, with each zone being 15 degrees in longitude wide. (The sun travels around the earth 360 degrees each day, and if you divide 360 by 24 hours, you get 15 degrees per hour.)

Dowd's system wasn't put into place until Sunday, November 18, 1883, a day that came to be known as "the day of the two noons." When the "new" noon arrived in each time zone, the U.S. Naval Observatory in Washington, D.C. telegraphed the time across the land. Any town east of the middle of a time zone had already experienced noon once; with the adoption of the Eastern, Central, Mountain, and Pacific time zones, the clocks in these towns struck noon once again.

While most people accepted the new time zones, some grew very upset, saying that the

idea of changing the time to accommodate the needs of businesses (specifically railroads) was an insult to their religious beliefs. We have always recorded time this way, they argued, and it's unnatural to change it.

These arguments have been made throughout history, with the most famous complaints coming from the adoption of the Gregorian calendar that wiped out 10

TRY, TRY AGAIN

Charles Dowd, a high school principal and professor of mathematics, is known as the father of time zones in the U.S., but he wasn't the first American to suggest a longitudinal solution to the problem of a hundred local time zones.

Back in 1809, amateur astronomer William Lambert recommended that Congress establish a prime meridian—that is, a longitude of degree 0—through Washington because our use of another country's prime meridian was "degrading" and "an encumbrance unworthy of the freedom and sovereignty of the American people and their government."

Along with this new prime meridian would come time zones 15 degrees wide to help citizens keep the hours in line. Congress rejected this proposal; one critic even called Lambert's idea "useless" because creating a new prime meridian would only force thousands of sailors to buy new maps!

Dowd had a much more practical goal than Lambert. Instead of trying to make the U.S. seem more important, he just wanted to make travel easy for everyone. With his time zone proposal in hand, he visited railway managers across the country in 1870 to see what they thought about the idea.

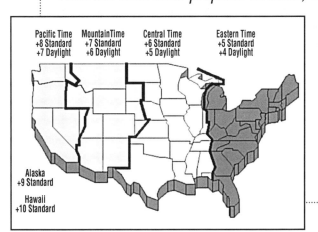

In 1872, Dowd issued a new plan to take account of everyone's suggestions. With the railroads supporting Dowd, it was only a matter of time before the U.S. made his time zones a reality.

days. For instance, when England switched to the Gregorian system in 1752—170 years after the rest of Europe—workers rioted, claiming that they had been cheated out of 10 days of pay when the calendars jumped from October 4 to October 15.

Of course these workers hadn't been cheated out of anything. It's true they weren't paid for those ten days, but they didn't work those ten days either. (As you've undoubtedly learned from your parents when you complained about

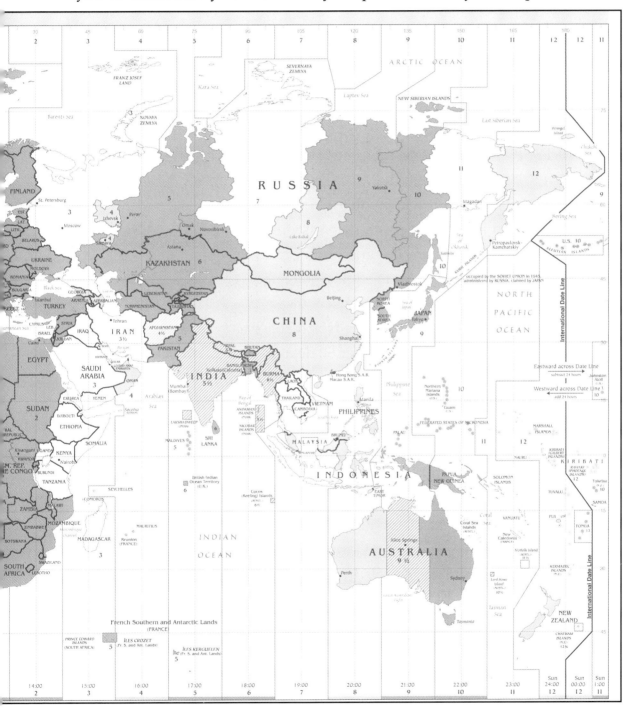

mowing the lawn, "No work, no pay.") The *calendar* lost ten days, not the workers. Calendars don't affect how time actually unrolls; they affect only how we look at time.

Zoning Out

In 1884, one year after the United States finally split its land into time zones, representatives from 25 countries met in Washington, D.C., to decide how to track time around the world. After much debate, the members of the International Meridian Conference decided to expand Charles Dowd's system to the entire globe, slicing the earth into vertical one-hour-wide time zones, each 15 degrees in longitude.

Everyone at the conference knew that global time zones were a good idea, but they strongly disagreed on where the prime meridian, the line of 0 degrees longitude, should be located. Mariners had long ago settled the issue of latitude; the equator, where the earth is the widest, was 0 degrees latitude, the North Pole was 90 degrees north, and the South Pole was 90 degrees south. End of story.

Longitude, however, remained a problem because you could place 0 degrees longitude on any vertical line on the globe and have your system work. Historically, the French had placed 0 degrees longitude at the Paris Observatory, while the British had placed it at the Greenwich Observatory, and so forth.

In the end, much to the disappointment of the French, the conference placed the prime meridian through the Greenwich Observatory. Greenwich had been issuing annual charts of the stars' movement for more than 100 years, which made Greenwich well known by world travelers.

Now, when it's noon in Greenwich, it's noon almost everywhere seven and a half degrees east or west of Greenwich as well. (France and Spain, for example, are at the same longitude as Greenwich, but these countries make their clocks match those of Germany, Italy, and most of Europe.) If you move west from Greenwich, the time will be one hour earlier for each 15 degrees you travel; if you move east, the time is one hour later. When it's 1 pm in Greenwich, the time is 5 am in Los Angeles; 7 am in Houston; 2 pm in Munich, Germany; and 11 pm in Sydney, Australia. Of course, daylight saving time throws a wrench into this well-timed machine.

There is one small problem with this system of time zones: If the time in Greenwich is 1 pm on Tuesday and you travel 12 time zones west, losing an hour for each zone, the local time is 1 am Tuesday; if, however, you travel 12 time zones

WHAT EXACTLY IS "ZULU TIME"?

If you've watched a military movie or followed the news closely, you may have heard the term "Zulu time." The name is misleading because it has nothing to do with how the members of the Bantu-speaking South African tribe keep track of their days.

In this case, "Zulu" is the military's way of saying "Z." Since radio and phone communication can be unclear—with "B" and "P" sounding similar, for instance, or "T," "D," and "V"—the military uses words to represent letters. If you live in apartment 4A, for example, you'd say that you live in apartment "four-Alpha."

The military labels each of the 24 time zones with its own letter. In the United States, the time zones are R (Romeo) for eastern, S (Sierra) for Central, T (Tango) for Mountain, U (Uniform) for Pacific, V (Victor) for Alaska, and W (Whiskey) for Hawaii. Zulu refers to time at the prime meridian, which we know as Greenwich mean time or GMT.

The U.S. military has bases and soldiers all over the globe, so it's much easier to issue commands in GMT and let each base figure out what GMT means in local time. Otherwise the military would take a lot longer to issue each command: "For those soldiers in flight on supersonic jets, the alert is for 1:45 pm, no, you just finished crossing the Rocky Mountains so it's 12:45 pm. But your final destination is the Philippines and that's five time zones away—or is it six?" Mission not accomplished . . .

east, gaining an hour for each zone, the local time is 1 am *Wednesday*.

Clearly something is wrong here. If you travel 12 time zones west from Greenwich on a jet and your friend travels east on a similar jet, your friend will not show up one day ahead of you. The two of you will arrive at the same time on the same day!

As with the switch to the Gregorian calendar, the confusion results from our attempt to *label* time, not from the passing of time itself. The earth, sun, and stars don't know whether it's Tuesday, Wednesday, or Grunsday. They just spin and spin and spin.

To solve this dating dilemma, the 180-degree line of longitude was dubbed the International Date Line. If you cross this line headed west, you jump ahead one day while keeping the hours and minutes the same; if you cross the line going east, you lose one day.

Believe it or not, before 1995 the International Date Line ran down the middle of the country of Kiribati. The eastern part of the country was one day and two hours behind the western part, which included the capital. In 1995, Kiribati shifted the International Date Line east so that the entire country would finally be on the same day.

Keep in mind that not all time zones are created equal. In the barren western areas of Russia, for example, many of the time zones are 30 degrees wide, which means you skip two hours when going from one to another. Iran, India, Afghanistan, and parts of Australia all have half time zones, so that when it's 1 pm in Greenwich, the time is 4:30 pm in Tehran and 6:30 pm in Bombay. Nepal is even trickier as it has its own time zone that's 5 hours and 45 minutes ahead of Greenwich.

China spreads across 60 degrees of longitude and could have five time zones, but the Chinese government chooses to use only one time zone for the entire country. This means the sun reaches its peak

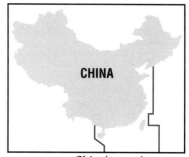

China's one time zone.

over the eastern part of the country at 11 am, while those in the west don't see "noon" until 3 pm—exactly the situation that the United States chose not to do. The working day for people living in western China starts long before sunrise, but some people choose to work untraditional hours so they don't have to get up in the middle of the night.

In general, the lines marking the time zones zigzag back and forth along the borders of countries, states, and cities as they go from the North Pole to the South Pole. They can do this because, once again, people created them, which means countries can decide what's best for them in a time zone and change it if it doesn't work.

TIME SAVED IS A PENNY EARNED

Although the first daylight saving time was in 1916, the idea dates back to 1784, when Benjamin Franklin wrote about moving hours around in an essay called "An Economical Project." Franklin lived in Paris at the time and had recently seen a new type of oil lamp demonstrated.

Benjamin Franklin

Discussion about the cost of oil led Franklin to write about how money could be saved if everyone both woke up and went to bed earlier. Franklin also joked about taxing windows with shutters and using church bells and even cannons to force people to adopt to the new system. "Oblige a man to rise at four in the morning," he wrote, "and it is probable he will go willingly to bed at eight in the evening."

Thankfully, instead of turning to heavy artillery to take advantage of the long daylight hours in spring and summer, we just move the hands of the clock—although we do remember our parents threatening to blast a cannon if we didn't get ready for school on time. Perhaps Ben Franklin did have the right idea!

If I Could Save Time in a Bottle . . .

Once everyone saw that the world didn't end when clocks changed to match the new time zones, they became a little more comfortable with the idea of moving time around. The next big clock change came when Germany and Austria set clocks ahead by one hour nationwide during the summer of 1916. The countries wanted to preserve fuel during World War I. Shifting the clocks moved an hour of sunlight from the morning to the evening, which meant that people used less electricity to light their homes.

Over the next year, most of the other European nations, as well as Australia and parts of Canada, also moved their clocks forward. The United States finally enacted a daylight saving law in 1918, but the government repealed the law after the end of the war because most citizens didn't like it. Even without this law,

AN IRON IN EVERY FIRE

Benjamin Franklin might be best known for the sayings that he created for Poor Richard's Almanack, *such as "A penny saved is a penny earned," but his contributions to the American colonies and the new country were immense.*

Over his lifetime, Franklin was—deep breath—a journalist, publisher, scientist, librarian, diplomat, inventor, author, philanthropist, and abolitionist (someone who argued for the elimination of slavery). Franklin was born in 1706 and had 16 siblings and half-siblings. His brother James started one of the first newspapers in Boston, but James didn't want Benjamin to help, so Benjamin wrote articles under a false name and slipped them under the print shop door at night. The articles became popular, but James was annoyed with his young brother and harassed him until he ran away.

Benjamin went to Philadephia, worked as an apprentice printer, then started

Massachusetts, Rhode Island, and a few cities including New York, Chicago, and Philadelphia continued daylight saving time (DST) during the summer months.

Daylight saving time, then called "war time," returned to the United States nationwide from 1942 to 1945 to help the country save fuel and energy for its troops in World War II. Once the war ended, the government got rid of the law once again, and states were free to either adopt daylight saving time or leave the clocks alone.

Unfortunately, some states adopted DST and some left their clocks alone, plunging the nation once again into a hodgepodge of local times, something

his own publishing shop. Over the next few years, he and his wife also ran a book store and a grocery store, started a newspaper, and began publishing Poor Richard's Almanack.

Throughout the 1730s and 1740s, Franklin organized campaigns to light, clean, and pave the streets of Philadelphia. He organized the city's first library and first volunteer firefighting company. He invented bifocals, swim fins, and a heat-efficient stove, now called the Franklin stove. In the 1750s, he experimented with electricity and discovered the true nature of lightning.

Franklin became involved in the movement for American separation from England and helped write the Declaration of Independence. After the American Revolution, he served as an ambassador to France, until he returned to the United

States to help write the U.S. Constitution.

Today, the memory of Benjamin Franklin is still honored through his presence on the $100 bill and the number of towns across the country named "Franklin."

WORDS TO KNOW

daylight saving time: *shifting the clock in the spring to gain an extra hour of daylight in the evening.*

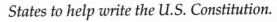

*Proposed new Atlantic Time
Zone including Maine.*

time zones were designed to end. Businesses begged for a solution to the confusion, but they didn't always beg for the same solution. Indoor theater owners, for example, argued for DST, while owners of drive-in theaters naturally wanted no DST so the sky would be darker earlier.

The solution finally came in 1966 when Congress passed the Uniform Time Act, which started DST nationwide at 2 am on the final Sunday in April and ended it at 2 am on the final Sunday in October. In 1986, the start date for DST moved to the first Sunday in April.

At the same time, however, Congress allowed states that include two time zones to opt out of DST. Currently, all of Hawaii and most of Arizona (everywhere but Native American reservations run by the Navahos) stay on standard time all year.

Now the state of Maine wants to switch from the Eastern Standard Time Zone to the Atlantic Standard Time Zone, so they'd be one hour earlier all the time, like staying on daylight saving time year round. Since Maine is the easternmost state on eastern time, it gets less evening daylight than any other state. The feeling is that by shifting more daylight from the morning to the evening people in Maine would save money on their energy costs and be able to pursue outdoor activities later in the day. Watch the news to see if Maine does move to a new time zone.

Indiana is a special case; most of the state ignores DST, staying on eastern standard time the whole year. However, five Indiana counties on the borders of Cincinnati, Ohio and Louisville, Kentucky use DST to stay in step with their large neighbors—and jump ahead an hour compared to the rest of the state. What's more, ten Indiana counties on the borders of Chicago and southern Illinois are actually in the Central Time Zone, and they spring ahead an hour to keep time with these areas, therefore matching up with the rest of the state just as the five eastern counties jump ahead.

The lesson to be learned here? Keep your windows rolled up as you drive through the Hoosier State and wait until you're over the border to find out what time it is.

CRYSTAL CLEAR TIMEKEEPING

Clocks and watches at the beginning of the twentieth century were incredibly accurate compared to the shadow clocks and klepsydras of ancient times. But horologists thought they could do even better.

After all, anything with moving parts eventually breaks down. Ride a bicycle every day for 50 miles and the chain will eventually come off; the more you drive a car, the greater the chance of getting a flat tire. Clocks have to do their thing night and day without a rest, so it's no surprise that springs come unsprung.

To make clocks work even better, horologists turned away from the gears and pendulums that had been used for the past 300 years and found inspiration

Discover the importance of quartz crystals

Learn the difference between analog and digital timekeeping

Apply accurate timekeeping to the world of sports

from an entirely new source: electricity. Of course, electricity itself wasn't new—lightning bolts had been striking the earth's surface for millions of years. But scientists who experimented with electricity kept finding out new facts about how it interacted with the rest of the world.

Around 1880, the French scientist Pierre Curie, working together with his brother Jacques, discovered that if you run an electric current through certain types of crystal, the crystal rapidly vibrates at a steady pace. The key words here are "at a steady pace" because one of the two elements you need in any clock

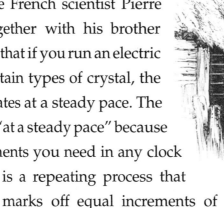

FRANKLIN'S EXPERIMENT WITH THE KITE.

See p. 46.

is a repeating process that marks off equal increments of time. By cutting the crystal in a particular shape, you can make it vibrate at a particular frequency.

Further research found that quartz crystals would be especially good for timekeeping since they vibrated at almost exactly the same rate—roughly 100,000 times per second—no matter what the temperature or air pressure.

Pierre Curie

To turn these vibrations into time, the electronic components of the watch make the vibrations larger (without changing the frequency), count them, and send a signal to the display each time the count passes 100,000 or so. In a quartz watch with hands, the

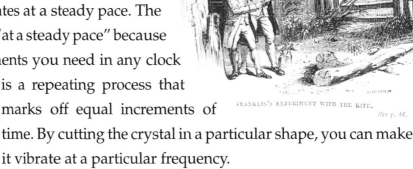

The quartz clock installed in the Greenwich Observatory in 1939 was accurate to within less than one second per year.

WORDS TO KNOW

piezoelectricity: *the electric current carried by quartz crystals.*

Curie point: *the temperature where a substance loses its magnetism.*

radioactivity: *the emission of a stream of particles or electromagnetic rays in nuclear decay.*

What radioactive elements did the Curies discover?

electronics make a pulse each second that drives a tiny motor, and this motor turns gears that drive the hands.

Joseph W. Horton and Warren A. Marrison first came up with the idea of using quartz crystals to make a clock in 1928, but quartz clocks didn't actually appear until the late 1930s. The decade-long wait was worth it to horologists due to the incredible accuracy of the quartz design. A clock installed in 1939

SCIENTISTS AND SUBJECTS

Most people like to receive awards and public recognition for their work. Pierre and Marie Curie were not like most people.

Pierre Curie, who was schooled at home by his physician father, was devoted to figuring out how the world worked and not interested in being famous. After

Pierre and Marie Curie

discovering piezoelectricity (the ability of quartz crystals to carry an electric current), Curie went on to study magnetism and figure out that at a certain temperature—now called the Curie point or Curie temperature—a substance loses its magnetic properties.

In 1895, Curie married Marie Sklodowska, and they spent much of the next decade studying radioactivity. In addition to creating the word "radioactive" to label substances like uranium, the Curies discovered two new radioactive elements: radium and polonium.

Today, we know that handling radium can make you very sick and cause cancer, but the Curies didn't know that. Pierre carried radium around in his coat pocket so that he could show friends what he was working on. Marie even kept a small pile of radium salt by her bed because she liked the way it glowed at night!

Thanks to dedicated scientists like these, the rest of us know more about the world—and when to keep parts of it a safe distance away from us . . .

How many times per second does a quartz crystal vibrate?

ONE HUNDRED HANDS TO BUILD A CLOCK WITH TWO

Horton and Marrison get all the credit for the first quartz crystal clock, but they succeeded thanks to the work of dozens of other scientists. Among the scientists Marrison mentions in a history of the crystal clock are:

- *John Shore, a trumpet player who invented the tuning fork in 1711 to help musicians keep the right note with their instruments.*

- *Jules Lissajouss, who demonstrated in 1857 that you can use electricity to make a tuning fork sound the same note for as long as you want.*

- *The Curie brothers, for their discovery in 1880 of piezoelectricity.*

- *H. M. Dadourian, who used a special motor in 1919 to count the number of cycles of sound a tuning fork made over a long period of time.*

- *J. A. Fleming and Lee DeForest, who in the early 1900s created different types of vacuum tubes, which use vibrations to transmit and amplify sound.*

- *W. H. Eccles, who combined vacuum tubes and tuning forks in 1919 to reduce friction and make the forks vibrate more steadily.*

- *Walter G. Cady, who in 1921 used quartz crystals to control the frequency of the vibrations in vacuum tubes.*

- *G. W. Pierce, who showed in 1923 that cutting quartz in particular ways lets you control how it vibrates.*

As Marrison wrote in his history, "It almost never happens that a result of any considerable value is obtained at a single stroke or comes through the efforts of a single person." No kidding, Mr. Marrison!

in the Greenwich Observatory in England kept time accurately to within two-one-thousanths of a second per day—that's less than one second of error over an entire year!

Like the first mechanical clocks that used escapements, early quartz clocks were huge and expensive, so while the timekeeping was very accurate, few people could afford one. Only in the 1970s did manufacturers figure out how to

Quartz crystal.

make a quartz design run on less power. Once they did this, they could fit the battery and quartz into a small wristwatch. In later years, as manufacturers learned to fit more power into even less space, quartz watches started featuring calculators, alarms, stop watches, and other features.

You can't see the vibrations of a quartz crystal unless you use a high-powered microscope. Analog quartz watches still have gears that use the quartz vibrations to move the hour, minute, and second hands, but they have fewer moving parts than analog watches of old that used a balance spring and winding stem. Fewer moving parts means less friction and fewer opportunities to break—an important advance from past designs.

Digital quartz watches, which first became available in the 1970s, use circuits to translate the quartz vibrations into an electronic display of the time. With no moving parts other than the vibrating quartz, they are extremely reliable—as long as you remember to take them off before you shower.

When Every Second (and Tenth of a Second) Counts

Athletic competition pits human against human in contests to see who can lift the most weight, who can throw an object the farthest, who can perform the most elegant gymnastic routine, or—most common of all—who is fastest. Skiing, swimming, skating, running, cycling: all of them are contests to see who can reach a goal in the shortest amount of time.

Some events are easy to compare. In the 100-meter dash, for instance, one person can fire a pistol to tell runners when to start running, while another person kneels next to the finish line to see who crosses it first.

This can be a good method, but if two (or more) runners are very close, you will have a hard time seeing which one finished first. In addition, not only do we care which athlete is the fastest today; we want to know whether an athlete today is faster than the one who won the race last time or the one forty years ago. We like to compare the performances of athletes over time, and we can do that only

What is the difference between analog and digital?

by keeping records of who took how long to do what.

Race officials also need to time events because not all athletes can compete at the same time. For instance, in the first American downhill ski races, organized by Norwegian and Swedish immigrants who moved to California during the gold

ANALOG VS. DIGITAL: WHAT'S THE DIFFERENCE?

An example of a digital clock is the standard bedside alarm clock with glowing red numbers that flashes 12:00 when the power comes back on after it has gone off. An analog clock might have a face with moving arms that point to the current hour, minute, and second. These clocks clearly differ from one another, but in what way do they differ the most?

Contrary to what you might think, it's not that all digital clocks are electric while all analog clocks are not. Many clocks with faces are plugged into an outlet or run on a battery, yet they're still analog.

The real difference comes in how a clock displays the time to a viewer. With a digital clock, time is displayed **discontinuously,** *which means that it appears in separate pieces or with breaks. The bedside clock reads 9:13 for a while, then suddenly changes to 9:14. Anyone who wants to know how many seconds passed while he waited for the minute to change is out of luck.*

Digital clocks can be more detailed, showing seconds, tenths of seconds, hundredths of seconds, and so on, but no matter how detailed you get, the clock still jumps from one reading of time to another.

Analog is the opposite of digital, which means that an analog clock displays time in a **continuous** *manner. As you watch the hands on an analog clock, you can see time pass before your eyes. If*

rush of the 1850s, all the skiers started at the same time, and the first one to reach the finish line won. The courses weren't set, so skiers could take any trail they wanted to get to the bottom.

Racers eventually decided this was unfair because some trails were better than others, so a fixed course was developed. Unfortunately, with everyone now taking the same trail, some skiers "accidentally" bumped others out of their

you watch for a while, you will see the hour hand move slowly from one number to another. The minute and second hands move more quickly, and by looking closely—and quickly—at these hands, you can see when it's fifteen minutes and three seconds past 4 o'clock and when it's fifteen minutes and three-and-one-half seconds past 4 o'clock.

Your senses act in an analog manner. For example, you can taste whether one pretzel is more or less salty than another, but you can't say precisely how much saltier it is. When you listen to music on a CD, you hear the music continuously, with notes and voices blending from one pitch to another—even though the music is encoded on the CD digitally, in thousands of separate electronic pieces that the stereo reads and recreates.

If you think about the timekeeping devices discussed in this book, you'll realize that most of them are analog. Shadow clocks, sundials, nocturnals, klepsydra, candle clocks, incense, pendulum clocks—all of them display time continuously as the sun moves, the water flows, and the wax melts.

Digital Sanglass??
,951; 8,952; 8,953; 8,954;

10,555 grains of sand

Interestingly, while the sandglass is analog, it could—with an awful lot of work—be turned into a digital clock. How? Take the sandglass apart and count the number of grains of sand, then put it back together and add a device to the sandglass that counts the grains as they fall from top to bottom. If the device displays the number of grains or percentage of grain that has fallen, you now have a digital clock!

What is the difference between analog and digital?

way—and with skiers moving up to 50 miles per hour, lots of damage could happen if you went off course.

To make sure skiers didn't hurt one another, racing officials switched to staggered starts, meaning skiers would start at different times and have their race times compared only after everyone was finished.

For decades, starting with the 1912 Olympic Games in Stockholm, Sweden, the only timing device available to athletes and race officials was the stopwatch. An official would press one button to start the stopwatch at the beginning of an event and press another button to stop it when someone crossed the finish line. This is an obvious way to track time, but it has two main problems.

First, to use a stopwatch, you have to be alert. If you sneeze at the start of the race, you might start the stopwatch late and make athletes seem a second or two faster than they really are. More importantly, the human reaction time has definite limits. You may see someone cross the finish line, but it takes a bit of time before your finger will press the button on the stopwatch. Another race official might be faster or slower than you, which means you can't compare times accurately.

The other problem with stopwatches is that they aren't accurate enough for many events. In the 1960s, for example, American Jim Hines held the world record for the 100-meter dash at 9.9 seconds. The stopwatches used at that time only measured tenths of a second, which means Hines actually took anywhere from 9.85 to 9.94 seconds. One-tenth of a second might not seem like much, but when the entire race takes less than 10 seconds, it's a big difference.

To solve these problems, race officials replaced humans holding stopwatches with computerized timing. The 1964 Olympics in Tokyo, Japan, for example, marked the first use of an electronic touch pad in swimming competitions and it proved to be valuable immediately. To the naked eye, the German Hans-Joachim Klein and the American Gary Ilman appeared to tie for third place in the 100-meter freestyle event. The timing devices showed that Klein had reached the touch pad a thousandth of a second before Ilman, however, so Germany was awarded the bronze medal.

Modern athletic events use photo-finish cameras that scan the finish line up to 2,000 times per second. As each athlete's chest crosses the finish line, the camera sends a message to the timing device.

Photo-finish cameras are a huge improvement over earlier measuring devices. In the 1932 Olympics in Los Angeles, American runners Eddie Tolan and Ralph Metcalfe were both timed at 10.3 seconds in the 100-meter dash. The tie wasn't broken until judges developed newsreel film of the race and examined individual frames of film to see that Tolan had won the race!

Timing devices are also used at the start of some events. In events like the 100-meter dash, runners start in a crouched position with their feet pressed against aluminum blocks. The blocks help the runners push off and start running faster, but they also electronically record when the athletes' feet leave the blocks. If anyone's feet leave the block within one-tenth of a second after the starting gun, the race official stops the race and has everyone start again. Our nerves and muscles just aren't fast enough to respond within one-tenth of a second, so anyone who started running before then must have started before the gun actually fired.

How were Olympic races timed in the early twentieth century?

ACTIVITY

Test Your Timing Reflex

Here's how to test your reflexes—and show how difficult it is to accurately time a race or other athletic event using a hand-held stopwatch.

For this activity you'll need two friends and two digital stopwatches. You and a friend each take a watch. The other friend will be the starter. When he or she says, "go!" start your stopwatch. When he or she says, "Stop!" hit the stop button. Now compare times with your friend. Are they the same? Imagine what it would be like if you were an Olympic athlete and you just happened to be timed by someone with slower reflexes than anyone else—goodbye, gold medal.

MEASURING TIME
WITHOUT MOVING

In the 1940s, despite its expense, quartz became the "go to" substance for time-keeping because quartz clocks were more accurate than any previous clock in human history. Within a decade, however, quartz was already old hat thanks to the arrival of atomic clocks.

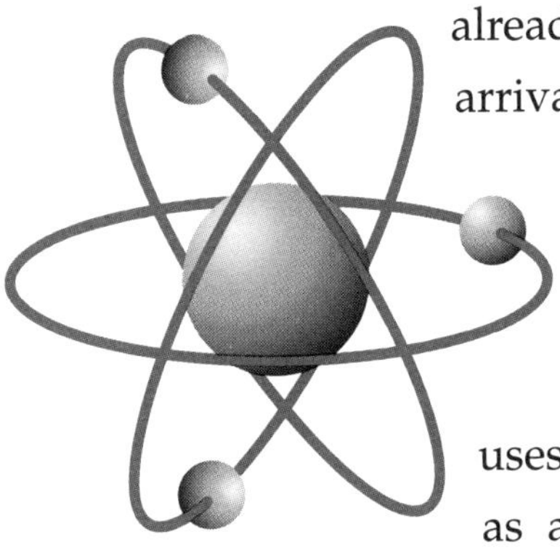

Scientists' understanding of atoms and molecules had come a long way by the mid-1900s. While some uses of atomic energy—such as atomic bombs and nuclear power plants—worried many people, other atomic developments benefited society in entirely safe ways.

Despite the name, an atomic clock cannot explode because it contains no radioactive or unstable elements. The first atomic clock, for example, which was designed in 1948 by

Learn how radio telescopes work

Discover how atomic clocks keep time

Find out how GPS is used in everyday life

WORDS TO KNOW

atomic clock: *an extremely accurate timekeeping device that is controlled by atomic or molecular vibrations.*

109

WAR-TIME DISCOVERY

During World War II, the physicist Harold Lyons and his co-workers at the National Bureau of Standards studied different frequencies of microwaves to try to improve the radar used by the American military.

You've probably used microwave energy only to heat food, but microwaves can be used for other purposes as well. If, for example, you shoot microwaves through a cloud of ammonia molecules—and the microwaves are at just the right frequency—some of the molecules will absorb energy from the microwaves and flip from one physical form to another, kind of like a hat being pushed inside out. The microwaves leaving the ammonia have less energy than when they entered.

Lyons already knew from the writings of fellow physicist Isidor Rabi that atoms of cesium would probably work better for timekeeping than molecules of ammonia, but he went ahead with ammonia due to his previous wartime experience with microwaves. Later atomic clocks worked far better than his ammonia clock, but Lyons still gets credit for being the first to harness atoms for timekeeping.

The first atomic clock.

Harold Lyons and built the following year by the U.S. National Bureau of Standards, used the vibration of ammonia molecules to control an electronic signal that displayed the time. This clock was ten times more accurate than a quartz clock, and that proved to be only the first of many improvements to come.

In 1955, Britain's National Physical Laboratory built an atomic clock

How long is a millisecond?

That is over 9 billion. . .count 'em. 9 BILLION.

The **Times Herald**

New Atomic Clock Uses Microwaves With a Frequency of 9,192,631,770 Cycles per Second

Who counted these cycles?

Lorem ipsum dolor sit amet, conse ctetuer adipiscing elit, sed diam no nummy nibh euismod tincidunt ut la creet dolore magna aliquam erat vo

Lorem ipsum dolor sit amet, conse ctetuer adipiscing elit, sed diam no nummy nibh euismod tincidunt ut la creet dolore magna aliquam erat vo

powered by atoms of cesium-133, a metallic element similar to mercury in that it's liquid at room temperature. In the clock, cesium atoms are heated, then sent through a magnetic field that allows only certain atoms to pass through. These atoms pass through a field of microwave energy that moves back and forth within a narrow range of frequencies, sort of like a radio that scans between 101.5 and 104.7, but more precise.

When the microwave energy has a frequency of exactly 9,192,631,770 Hertz (Hz, or cycles per second), any cesium atoms hit by the microwaves change to a different energy state. The changed cesium atoms reinforce the microwaves so that their frequency always remains at 9,192,631,770 Hz. Once this happens, another device within the clock translates this frequency into the familiar one beat per second that we all know and love.

What's most amazing about this clock is that it had an error rate of only one second every 300 years—which is actually more precise than the solar system itself! How can this be? Well, you might have the idea that the earth uses "cruise control" in its travels, that it always moves at the same rate as it orbits the sun. In fact, because the earth's orbit is an ellipse and not a circle, the earth moves faster when it's close to the sun and slower when it's far away.

But wait, there's more! The earth doesn't always spin on its axis at the same rate. Strong, consistent winds and the pressure of the atmosphere can cause the earth to slow down, increasing the length of a day by a fraction of a millisecond (one-thousandth of a second). The

WORDS TO KNOW

cesium-133: *a metalic element that is liquid at room temperature.*

microwave energy: *electromagnetic energy with a wavelength longer than infrared light but shorter than radio waves.*

ellipse: *an oval-shaped figure.*

Hertz: *cycles per second.*

Why doesn't the earth always spin at the same rate?

daily movement of the tides is also slowing the earth by about 1.4 milliseconds per day over a hundred-year period.

That might not sound like much, but those 1.4 milliseconds add up over time. As scientists found out more about the movement of the earth and how it changes over time, they decided that they could no longer define a second as 1/86,400 of a solar day (with a solar day being the period from noon to noon, and 86,400 seconds equaling 1,440 minutes, which equals 24 hours).

Instead, in 1967 at the Thirteenth General Conference on Weights and Measures, the second was redefined as (take a deep breath), "the duration of 9,192,631,770 periods of the radiation corresponding to the transition between the two hyperfine levels of the ground state of the cesium-133 atom."

In other words, you can measure atoms more precisely than planets, an idea that only makes sense the more you think about it. After all, which can you measure more accurately: the length of your finger or of a car, the height of a chair or of the flagpole at your school? The longer, higher, or bigger something is, the more likely you are to make an error while measuring it—and it might not even be your fault. The wind might move the flagpole, for instance, and that will throw off your accuracy.

Keeps On Ticking

A clock that loses or gains only one second over 300 years sounds pretty good, but for scientists it was only the beginning of fifty years of improvement. In 1975, for example, NBS-6—a cesium clock run by the National Bureau of Standards (NBS)—improved the error rate to one second every 300,000 years. By 1993, the National Institute of Standards and Technology (NIST—the new name for NBS) had created a clock 20 times better than NBS-6.

In 1999, while most of the world worried about their computers losing track of 100 years due to the "millennium bug," NIST introduced NIST-F1,

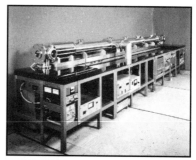

Top: NBS-6
Bottom: NIST-F1

a cesium fountain atomic clock that will not gain or lose a second in more than 20 million years!

Now, a couple of questions probably come to mind about NIST-F1: **How can we possibly know that the clock is that accurate?** Instead of counting, scientists have learned enough about cesium, lasers (which shoot "balls" of cesium up and down like a fountain), physics, and the design of the clock to know where errors might show up and how bad those errors will be. Just as quartz watches eliminated errors in timekeeping caused by friction and faulty springs, the next generation of atomic clocks will be designed to eliminate those errors that still exist in NIST-F1.

Why in the world do we need clocks that precise? Scientists often research subjects just because they're interesting and fun, not because the results of the research can make lots and lots of money. They do the research first, then let other people worry about whether it's useful or not.

As it turns out, making very accurate clocks has allowed scientists and manufacturers to do all sorts of things that weren't possible before. Today's computer networks can "read" atomic time over the Internet so that they all have the correct time, which is important for proper communication between computers.

Astronomers use radio telescopes orbiting the earth to try to "see" far into the universe. By using atomic time, they can link these telescopes together to get a more accurate picture of galaxies and quasars billions of light years away.

GPS: Gonna Pinpoint Something

The most important use of atomic clocks to date has to be the Global Positioning System (GPS), a set of 24 satellites that orbit the earth. Each of these satellites takes 12 hours to make a complete orbit, and they're arranged in space so that every point on the planet is always in radio contact with at least four satellites.

The GPS satellites constantly send radio waves toward the earth, and anyone with a GPS receiver can pick up these signals. As the signals travel toward earth, they change frequency depending on where someone is in relation to the satellite. If the satellite is moving toward you, the radio signal will increase in frequency

Approximately how many seconds in a day?

Visit **http://nist.time.gov** to see the correct time in your neck of the woods.

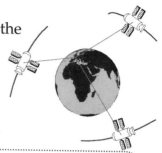

because it's covering slightly less ground to reach you; once the satellite passes overhead, its frequency will slightly decrease because the satellite is now moving away from you.

This effect is called the Doppler shift, and you have probably already experienced this change in frequency from

USING CLOCKS TO IMPROVE YOUR VISION

To understand how clocks help scientists see better, hold your hand over one eye and look around the room. Everything will look flatter than normal because you're seeing it from only one angle. Uncover your eye and look again; the room should return to normal. What's happening is that your brain takes the images from the two eyes and blends them into one, letting you more accurately judge how far away different objects are.

Now imagine that your internal clock isn't working right, and your right eye processes information one second slower than the left. If you try to play baseball, you'll see two images of the ball because you're seeing them at different times. Hope you're wearing a helmet!

While you're limited to using information from two eyes, astronomers can use any number of radio telescopes as long as the information they see comes at the exact same point in time. Atomic clocks allow this level of precision, so astronomers have been able to link ten telescopes between Hawaii and the Virgin Islands to create, in effect, a 5,000-mile-wide telescope. This allows astronomers to learn more about the parts of the universe farthest away from us.

WORDS TO KNOW

Global Positioning System: *a system of satellites, computers, and receivers that is able to determine the latitude and longitude of a receiver on earth by calculating the time difference for signals from different satellites to reach the receiver.*

Sputnik: *world's first satellite, launched by the Soviet Union in 1957.*

listening to a fire engine or ambulance as it passed you on the street. As the vehicle approaches you, its siren or bell sounds like it's getting higher and higher—and the moment it passes you, the sound drops lower and keeps falling.

The day after the Soviet Union launched Sputnik in 1957, researchers at MIT were able to calculate the satellite's orbit by tracking its Doppler shift. The U.S. Navy picked up on this idea and launched its first attempt at a satellite

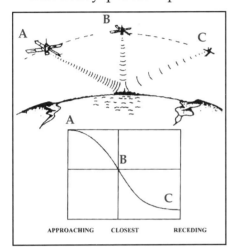

navigation system in 1965. The six satellites in the Transit System sent radio signals to American submarines carrying Polaris nuclear missiles and provided the submarines with such accurate signals that the subs were able to stay submerged in the ocean for months at a time—something they couldn't previously do without getting far off course.

The idea for GPS came at a brainstorming session at the Pentagon in 1973. The Department of Defense had already successfully launched a few, small-scale satellite navigation systems, so why not try something bigger, something that would cover the entire world? The first GPS satellite was launched in 1978, and the final one in 1993; each satellite weighs about 1,900 pounds and carries four atomic clocks on board. GPS first gained wide public attention in the 1991 Gulf War, when U.S. troops used GPS signals to find their way through the empty deserts of the Middle East and target bombs accurately.

Like many technological innovations that were first developed for the military, GPS has been adopted for many other uses:

- GPS installed in vehicles tells drivers where they are instantly. GPS systems can even speak directions so drivers never have to take their eyes off the road. Boat owners use GPS to help them navigate.

- Earth scientists use GPS to keep track of earthquakes and monitor the shifting of the earth's crust. In the future, we might be able to predict when and where an earthquake will occur, something we can only guess at today.

How does GPS work?

- Transportation companies use GPS in their truck and airplane fleets so that they can estimate when goods will reach their customers.

- To catch thieves, sheriffs' departments have placed GPS systems inside expensive cars and left the cars unlocked to serve as bait. If a car is stolen, an officer can follow the car on a monitor and find out where the thief lives.

- Airlines use GPS to make flight paths more efficient, saving time and money. Pilots can make safer landings because they know their exact position in the air.

- Civil engineers use GPS to map and measure the earth, lay out paths for future roads, track forest fires, and guide bulldozers during construction.

- Pet owners can have a tiny GPS tag placed under the skin of their animal so that if their pet runs away or gets lost, they can easily find them.

ACTIVITY

Finding a Quarter in a Haystack

You can see for yourself how GPS works by getting together with three friends and performing a few experiments. If you need to entice them, let them know the experiment is all about finding money in a field.

Your friends get to play the role of the GPS satellites; position them at the edges of a large grassy field (approximately football-field size with long grass that hides the ground), roughly at equal distances from one another. Have them slowly walk around the field, looking inward at the field the entire time. At some point, throw a quarter through the air so that it lands in the middle of the field. If the "satellites" have been doing their jobs, they'll be able to pool their information together ("It landed to my left." "It landed at least fifteen feet away from where I was.") and find the quarter.

Not convinced? Have one person walk around the edge of the field and repeat the experiment. The "satellite" will have a general indication of where the coin landed, but will likely have to spend much more time searching for the coin. An expensive experiment, perhaps, but now you'll have an idea how GPS works!

TIME ON YOUR HANDS

By looking at the history of timekeeping, we have also learned about the history of time itself: what it is and isn't, and how time has become an essential part of our modern world.

More importantly, we've gained an idea of how timekeeping and our ideas of time affect one another. If we divide a length of time a particular way—24 hours in a day, for example, or 60 seconds in a minute—we will design timekeeping devices to track those pieces. If we create a timekeeping device that's more accurate than our current divisions—such as an atomic clock that counts cesium's 9,192,631,770 pulses—we will divide time into smaller pieces to match what we are capable of tracking.

Time is as much a tool in our society as a hammer or stapler, and we use time zones and daylight saving time to make time a more useful tool. We add days to calendars and leap seconds

See how time can be measured in whole new ways

Meet Einstein and understand the theory of relativity

Create your own unique calendar

to the year. We manipulate time by setting our watch five minutes ahead so that we arrive at appointments early.

One time trick we haven't tried (yet) is a reorganization of the whole shebang: days, months, minutes, years, everything. Why would we want to do that? Well, we divide a year into 365 pieces (and sometimes 366), months into 28–31 pieces, a day into 24 pieces, an hour into 60 pieces, and a second into hundreds or millions of pieces. No unit of time relates easily to another, so the system is hard to learn and even harder to calculate using our base 10 counting system. How many days is 1,000,000 minutes? How many years is 10,000 days? Get out the calculator and start punching buttons!

"The Time at the Tone is Twenty-Five O'Clock"

Measuring time doesn't have to be so complicated. For example, J. William Cupp, an associate professor of computer and information sciences at Indiana Wesleyan University, has proposed a system for metric time that makes counting much easier. He keeps the solar day and solar year but changes everything else. Under his system, the day is broken up into 25 hours with each hour having 100 minutes and each minute 100 seconds.

25 metric hours in a day

100 metric minutes in a metric hour

100 metric seconds in a metric minute

If you do the math, our current system has 86,400 seconds in a day (24 hours x 60 minutes x 60 seconds); under Cupp's system, a day lasts 250,000 metric seconds, so each metric second is about one-third of a regular second. Similarly, each metric minute is about half of a regular minute.

Cupp did this so that adopting a metric time system would be fairly easy. If you microwave a bag of popcorn, set the timer for 8 minutes instead of 4; a 3-minute egg becomes a 6-minute egg without spending a moment longer in the water. A metric hour is equal to 57.6 of today's minutes, and who's likely to notice the loss of 2.6 minutes?

Like Marco Mastrofini (who we talked about in chapter one), Cupp proposes a calendar in which every month starts on a Sunday so that people can use the same calendar every year instead of having to buy a new one. Each month would have 28 days, and a year would have 13 months with one special New Year's Day that falls between December 28 and January 1.

While it makes sense to have timekeeping be as easy as possible, changing over to Cupp's system would take a lot of work. Every watch and clock, every cell phone and PDA, every calendar and day timer—every business transaction in the world—would have to be changed. Building the Great Wall of China would look like a kindergarten Tinkertoy project in comparison, traveling to the moon would seem like a walk to the store to buy eggs, splitting the atom no harder than spreading jam on a bagel!

A lot of work, yes, but we've taken on such projects before. In 1999, the world overhauled computers to avoid the "millennium bug" that would crash everything on January 1, 2000. In 2002, twelve European countries—roughly 300 million people—threw out their old currencies and adopted an entirely new system of money, the Euro.

In fact, after the French Revolution in 1793, the French government used a metric time system for the next 13 years. The revised calendar had 12, three-week-long months, with each week having 10 days. Each solar day was broken into 10 metric hours, each hour into 100 metric minutes, and each minute into 100 metric seconds. Most of the metric system created during the French Revolution—meters, liters, and grams—has spread throughout the world, but metric time didn't make it.

WORDS TO KNOW

millennium bug: *the inability of computer software and hardware to recognize the century change in a date.*

Why would it be difficult to change to a metric time system? Why would we want to?

ACTIVITY

Dawn of a New Day

What if you had the chance to throw out the old calendars and clocks and design a completely new way to keep time? How would you do it? You might want to make July and August 80 days long so you have more time off from school, but parents and principals would probably just hold classes in the summer. You can't trick them that easily!

Keep in mind that most of our timekeeping system is arbitrary; ancient civilizations chose something hundreds or thousands of years ago, and we still do it the same way because that's how we learned it. What if you could do anything you want, though? Would you still make a year equal to one revolution of the earth around the sun? A day equal to one rotation of the earth so that it again faces the sun?

What's important to you in a calendar or the hours of a day? Try to imagine a system unlike either our current one or Cupp's metric calendar. How creative can you be and still have the hours and days add up? Draw your new calendar and keep track of it as the days pass (*your* days, mind you, in case you created something other than a 24-hour day) to see how well your creation works as time marches on.

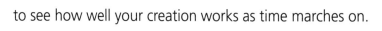

So what do you think? Which timekeeping system should we have: the clunky 24-hour clock that we all know and understand, or a funky new 25-hour system that would be easy to learn and make adding minutes and hours easier?

Time Flies

As we go about our daily lives, physical objects don't normally affect how quickly or slowly time passes. If your living room clock stops working, time keeps on going; the clock doesn't create time but only measures it. Once you get the clock

EVERY YEAR TELLS A STORY

Sometimes folks create new calendars to fix the mistakes of the past—but sometimes they do it just to create something new. Chris Hardman, the artistic director of a theater company in Sausalito, California, falls in the second category. Unlike most calendars, Hardman's "ECOlogical Calendar" unfolds as one long sheet, beginning with the winter solstice, December 21, instead of January 1. In addition to using the standard names of the days, Hardman gives each day an individual name relating to the weather: February 17 is "FreezeSleep," while the next two days in February are named "ArcticAir" and "QuickCold."

The illustrations on the calendar show the seasons flowing into one another, and Hardman uses the names of the days to tell a story that emphasizes how the days and months flow together over time. For example, the sentence covering February 17–19 reads:

"FreezeSleep comes to woolly bear caterpillars as ArcticAir blows toward the equator making QuickCold all things outside."

Hardman's idea is to do away with the seven-day week and return to a better awareness of nature and the larger world. Do you think this calendar can make that happen?

repaired, you can ask a neighbor for the time and reset your clock because time passes the same for your neighbor as it does for you.

Or does it? As Albert Einstein explained in his 1905 essay on relativity, the answer is sometimes no. Einstein's essay turned the world of science upside-down because it destroyed the idea of an "absolute time" that exists outside the physical happenings of the

WORDS TO KNOW

relativity: *the idea that an object's movement and speed make sense only when compared with other objects.*

SEEKER OF SOLAR SECRETS

Albert Einstein is the world's most famous scientist—despite the fact that most people can't understand what he discovered!

Einstein, born in 1879 in Germany, lived in Italy and Switzerland when he was young. After finishing college, he couldn't find a teaching position, so he took a job as an assistant in the Swiss Patent Office. During this time, he published physics papers that threw the world of science into a tizzy. His theory of special relativity, which described how particles move when traveling near the speed of light, included

Albert Einstein, taken by Yousef Karsh, February 1948.

the formula $E=mc^2$, which shows that energy is equal to mass multiplied by the speed of light (186,000 miles per second squared).

His second most famous paper introduced the theory of general relativity, which explained that acceleration (an increase in motion, such as when you push on the gas pedal) is equal to the force of gravity (the "pull" that large objects generate, such as the earth's pull on objects on its surface). If, for example, you rode on an extremely fast rocket ship, the speed of the ship would push you towards the back wall, just like the gravity of earth pushes you into the ground.

Einstein left Germany in 1933 for political reasons and moved to the United States. In 1939, he wrote to President Roosevelt about the possibility of using uranium to make bombs of enormous power, while warning that Germany was probably already trying to create such bombs. After the U.S. used hydrogen bombs on Hiroshima and Nagasaki, Einstein was horrified by the results and became a leading figure in the World Government Movement. As he said, "He who cherishes the values of culture cannot fail to be a pacifist."

universe. Instead, Einstein argued that everyone has his or her own personal time, a time related to your movement.

Relativity is hard to wrap your head around, but Einstein showed that time passes at the same rate for two people only if they are moving in the same direction and at the same speed, such as being passengers in the same taxi or riding a bicycle built for two. If, however, the two people move at different rates of speed or in different directions or both, then their "personal clocks"—the rate at which time passes for each of them—will not necessarily match. Their clocks might differ by only the tiniest amount, but they will differ.

Believe it or not, this wacky-sounding idea has been proven in numerous experiments. In October 1971, for instance, cesium-based atomic clocks were flown around the world both from east to west and from west to east. Atomic clocks set to the same time were left in place at the U.S. Naval Observatory. After making the trips, researchers compared the clocks and found that the clocks

−59 nanoseconds

+273 nanoseconds

that went east to west *lost* an average of 59 nanoseconds (a nanosecond is a billionth of a second) and those going from west to east *gained* an average of 273 nanoseconds.

Why did one clock gain time while the other lost it? Did one clock pick the other's pocket? In fact, the answer involves both speed and gravity, the force that keeps us from flying into space.

Einstein found that as you travel faster, anyone looking at you from outside your vehicle will see you as moving more slowly. If, for example, you flew on a spaceship at nearly the speed of light (186,000 miles per second) and made a round trip to the star Alpha Centauri, when you got back to earth your clock would be far behind the clocks on earth. Nine years might have passed on earth between the moment you left and the moment you returned, but for you the trip took only, say, six years.

Everyone on earth will think that your clock ran slow and lost three years during the trip. You, on the other hand, will think that the clocks on earth ran fast and gained three years. As relativity explains, you're both correct!

While on the spaceship at near light speed, you would feel time pass at the same rate it always has. A clock would tick, tick, tick just like normal. Only after you return home would you learn that less time passed on the spaceship than passed on earth. If you had a twin sister who stayed on earth during your trip, your twin would now be three years older than you!

The World in Motion

The key to relativity comes from Einstein's discovery that people are wrong to think that some objects stay in place while other objects move. Everything moves—planets orbit stars, stars orbit the center of the galaxy, galaxies move through space—but from the point of view of each object, that object is fixed while the universe moves around it.

If you walk past a friend on the sidewalk, for example, you can imagine that you are staying in place and your friend (and the sidewalk, the buildings, and the rest of the city) is moving past you; your friend, of course, can do the same thing. If you've ever been on a train, you might have already experienced this sensation. Sometimes when you look out the window, you can't tell whether your train is moving forward, the train next to you is moving backward, or both trains are moving at the same time.

Again, from Einstein's point of view, all three points of view are correct. Riders on both trains can imagine that their train is staying still while the other

train is moving, and someone standing beside the tracks will say that both trains move. An object's movement and speed make sense only when compared with other objects, and as a result time passes differently for each object.

As Einstein later revealed in his General Theory of Relativity, published in 1915, gravity also affects the rate at which time passes by, "curving" both space and time. The more massive an object is, the more that space-time—Einstein's

> **gravity . . . affects the rate at which time passes by, "curving" both space and time**

name for our physical universe—curves around it. In 1919, British scientists saw that stars near the sun appeared to shift during an eclipse. The stars' light was normally "bent" by the sun, but during the eclipse people on earth could see the light in an "unbent" form. Einstein was proven correct and again shook up the world of science.

Time is relative, but in general, we can ignore this little quirk of the universe. We live on a planet that rotates at up to 1,000 miles per hour (depending on where you are on the earth's surface) and moves around the sun at 18.5 miles per second. Our solar system moves through the Milky Way galaxy at 155 miles per second, and the Milky Way galaxy is moving among other nearby galaxies at 185 miles per second. So it hardly matters if you drive five miles an hour faster than someone else on the highway—your wristwatches

WORDS TO KNOW

space-time: *what Einstein called the physical universe.*

aren't precise enough to track time by nanoseconds!

To return to our spaceship example, on a round trip to Alpha Centauri you would "lose" three years when compared with everyone on earth—but if you never returned to earth, you'd never know that. On board the spaceship, you'd age at the same rate and clocks—whether shadow clocks, klepsydra, or quartz watches—would run at the same rate.

Time is a personal thing, one we hope you'll explore more in the years ahead.

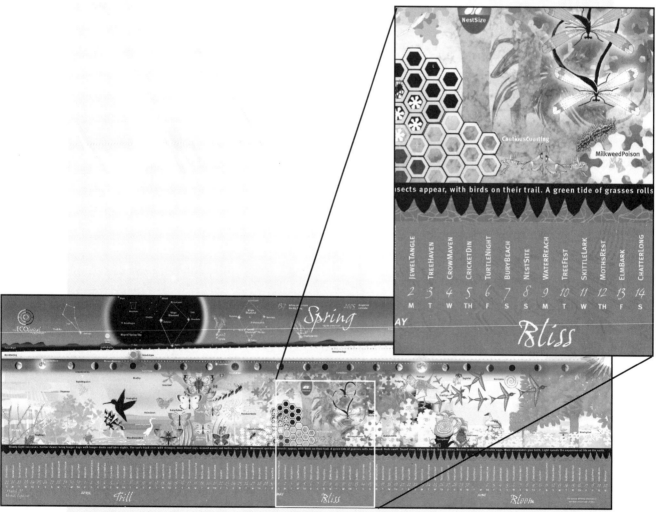

ECOlogical Calendar.

GLOSSARY

analog clock: time is displayed in a continuous manner.

anchor escapement: an escapement shaped like an anchor that made pendulum clocks more accurate.

apeiron: a Greek word meaning unending, unlimited mass.

astrolabe: a device that measures the altitude of the sun or a star to determine latitude.

atomic clock: an extremely accurate timekeeping device that is controlled by atomic or molecular vibrations.

axis: the center around which something rotates.

base 10 counting system: a number system based on units of 10.

base 60 counting system: a number system based on units of 60.

BCE: before the common era, a modern term for BC, Before Christ.

Big Dipper: see Ursa Major.

cesium-133: a metallic element that is liquid at room temperature.

chronometer: a very accurate timepiece used in navigation to determine longitude.

clock: comes from the French word *cloque*, which means bell.

constellation: group of stars.

Curie point: the temperature where a substance loses its magnetism.

daylight saving time: shifting the clock in the spring to gain an extra hour of daylight in the evening.

degrees: a measure for arcs and angles; sections of a circle.

digital clock: time is displayed discontinuously, in separate pieces

Doppler shift: the change in frequency when a source and observer are in motion relative to each other. The frequency increases when the source and observer approach each other and decrease when they move apart.

ellipse: an oval-shaped figure.

epagomenal days: days outside of the regular Egyptian calendar.

equator: a line around the middle of the earth that's equally far from the North and South Poles.

equinox: the day in spring (March 20, 21, or 22) or fall (September 20, 21, or 22) when the number of hours of daylight and nighttime are equal and the sun rises directly in the east and sets directly in the west.

escapement: a device that regulates short periods of time so they are always the same length.

fathom: a unit of measure equaled to six feet used to measure marine depths. Comes from the old English meaning "outstretched arms," essentially the distance between the fingers of outstretched arms.

foliot: a lever with weighted arms attached to the paddled rod of the verge escapement.

fusee: a spiral pulley used to even out the power of a mainspring in a watch.

Global Positioning System (GPS): a system of satellites, computers, and receivers that is able to determine the latitude and longitude of a receiver on earth by calculating the time difference for signals from different satellites to reach the receiver.

gnomon: a vertical device that casts a shadow on some sort of ruler or measuring stick to keep track of time.

grasshopper escapement: an escapement developed by John Harrison that made clocks more accurate.

Gregorian calendar: the calendar revised by Pope Gregory XIII in 1582, which is still in use today.

haab: a Mayan solar calendar.

Hertz: cycles per second.

horologist: someone who makes clocks and watches.

horology: the art of designing and making clocks.

incense: a slow-burning substance that produces a fragrant odor when burned.

International Date Line: an imaginary line that zigs and zags through the Pacific Ocean (to avoid going through any land) that is at 180 degrees longitude. On the west side of the line it is one day later than on the east side. It is where 180 degrees west meets 180 degrees east.

Julian calendar: calendar created by Julius Caesar in 45 BCE.

klepsydra: a clock that tracks time using dripping water; also called a water glass.

knot: a unit of speed—one nautical mile per hour.

latitude: a measure of how far north or south of the equator you are located.

Little Dipper: see Ursa Minor.

longitude: north-south lines circling the globe, running through the North and South Poles, also called meridians; a measurement of how far a location is east or west of the prime meridian.

lunar: relating to or associated with the moon.

lunar month: the time from one new moon to the next, 29.5 days.

meridian: a line around the earth that goes through the North and South Poles; another word for noon from Latin *meri* (middle) and *diem* (day).

microwave energy: electromagnetic energy with a wavelength longer than infrared light but shorter than radio waves.

millennium bug: the inability of computer software and hardware to recognize the century change in a date.

nocturnal: a device that tells time at night using the stars.

North Star: see Polaris.

Northern Hemisphere: north of the equator.

pendulum clock: a clock using a swinging pendulum to move its gears.

piezoelectricity: the electric current carried by quartz crystals.

Polaris: the North Star, which lies directly over the North Pole.

prime meridian: the north-south line running between the North and South Poles through Greenwich, England, set as 0 degrees longitude.

quadrant: a measuring instrument for measuring altitude used to determine latitude; a quarter of the circumference of a circle.

radioactivity: the emission of a stream of particles or electromagnetic rays in nuclear decay.

railway time: a standard time used by railroads that stayed the same, regardless of location.

relativity: the idea that an object's movement and speed make sense only when compared with other objects.

shadow clock: a clock developed by Ancient Egyptians that uses the sun's shadow to track time; also called a time stick.

sidereal day: how long it takes the earth to rotate once on its axis.

siphon: a tube running from the liquid in a vessel to a lower level outside the vessel so that atmospheric pressure forces the liquid through the tube.

solar: relating to or associated with the sun.

solar day: how much time passes between noon and noon.

Southern Hemisphere: south of the equator.

space-time: what Einstein called the physical universe.

Sputnik: the world's first satellite, launched by the Soviet Union in 1957.

summer solstice: the date with the longest day and the shortest night of the year. This is June 21 or 22 in the Northern Hemisphere; December 21 or 22 in the Southern Hemisphere.

sundial: tells time by the shadow that the gnomon casts on a calibrated dial.

time stick: see shadow clock.

time zone: one of the 24 regions of the globe; loosely divided by longitude, within which the same standard time is used.

tzolkin: a Mayan calendar consisting of 260 days.

Ursa Major: the most conspicuous of the constellations in the northern sky. It is near the North Pole and contains 53 visible stars, seven of which form the Big Dipper.

Ursa Minor: one of the northernmost constellations. It contains 23 visible stars, including those forming the Little Dipper. The most important of these stars is the North Star.

verge escapement: clock escapement that uses vertical rods with paddles.

winter solstice: the date with the shortest day and the longest night of the year. This is December 21 or 22 in the Northern Hemisphere and June 21 or 22 in the Southern Hemisphere.

zenith: highest point; directly overhead.

RESOURCES

Books

Chapman, Gillian and Pam Robson. <u>Exploring Time</u>. Millbrook Press, 1994.

Collier, James Lincoln. <u>Clocks</u>. Benchmark Books, 2004.

Dale, Rodney. <u>Timekeeping</u>. Oxford University Press, 1992.

Humphrey, Henry and Deirdre O'Meara-Humphrey. <u>When Is Now?</u> Doubleday & Company, 1980.

Landes, David S. <u>Revolution in Time</u>. Harvard University Press, 1983.

Lippincott, Kristen. <u>The Story of Time</u>. Merrell Holberton, 1999.

Williams, Brian. <u>Latitude & Longitude</u>. Smart Apple Media, 2003.

Web Sites

National Maritime Museum, Greenwich, UK: <u>www.nmm.ac.uk</u>

Site devoted to calendar reform:
<u>http://personal.ecu.edu/mccartyr/calendar-reform.html</u>

Encyclopedia Brittanica Online history of time:
<u>www.britannica.com/clockworks</u>

U.S. Naval Observatory: <u>www.usno.navy.mil</u>

National Watch and Clock Museum: www.nawcc.org/museum

National Institute of Standards and Technology: <u>www.nist.gov</u>

For local time: <u>http://nist.time.gov</u>

U.S. Naval Observatory: <u>http://aa.usno.navy.mil/</u>

<u>www.timeanddate.com</u>

<u>www.greenwichmeantime.com</u>

To find your latitude: U.S. Geological Survey: <u>http://geonames.usgs.gov/</u>

INDEX

Alexander the Great: 17, 20

analog: 99, 103–105

Anaximander: 20, 21

Andronicus: 38, 39

astrolabe: 44, 45

atomic clock: 109–115, 117, 123

Babylonians: 5, 6, 15–17, 20, 22

base 10 counting system: 17, 19, 20, 118

base 60 counting system: 17, 19, 20

Bernard of Verdun: 45

Big Dipper: 24, 48–50

Caesar, Julius: 8-11

calendar: 5–11, 14–16

candle clock: 51–54, 59, 66, 68, 105

Cassiopeia: 48–50

cesium: 110–113, 117, 123

China, Chinese: 14, 40, 41, 54, 61, 94, 95

chip log: 42

chronometer: 79, 80, 82

Congreve, Sir William: 55, 56

constellations: see stars

Copernicus, Nicolas: 73

Cupp, J. William: 118–120

Curie, Marie: 101

Curie, Pierre: 100–102

Curie point: 100, 101

daylight saving time: 93, 95–98, 117

digital: 99, 103–105, 108

Dondi, Giovanni de: 67

Doppler shift: 114, 115

Dowd, Charles: 88, 89, 92

Eastern Hemisphere: 81, 82

ECOlogical Calendar: 121, 126

Egyptians: 5, 6, 15–18, 20, 35, 37, 41, 51, 60

Einstein, Albert: 117, 121, 122, 123, 124, 125

equator: 10, 13, 21–23, 44, 45, 76, 77, 92

escapement: 62–68, 70–72, 75–77, 79, 102

Flamsteed, Reverend John: 87

foliot: 64, 65, 68, 70

Franklin, Benjamin: 95–97

fusee: 71

Galilei, Galileo: 62, 69, 72–75, 86, 87

gnomon: 19–22, 32, 33, 81

GPS (Global Positioning System): 109, 113–117

Greek, Greeks: 17, 20, 22, 35, 38, 41, 44

Greenwich, England: 77, 78, 81, 82, 86, 92, 94

Greenwich mean time (GMT): 88, 93

Gregorian calendar: 10, 11, 14, 89, 90, 94

Hardman, Chris: 121

Harrison, John: 79, 80, 86

Henlein, Peter: 70, 71

Hertz: 111

Honnecourt, Villard de: 63–65

Horton, Joseph W.: 101, 102

hourglass: 41–44, 66, 68, 69, 105

Huygens, Christian: 75, 76

incense clock: 51, 52, 54, 55, 58, 59, 105

International Date Line: 82, 94

International Meridian Conference: 92

Kendall, Larcum: 80

klepsydra: 35–42, 51, 59, 61, 66–68, 99, 105, 126

King Charles II: 86, 87

knot: 44

Lambert, William: 89

latitude: 15, 22–26, 44, 56, 57, 77, 78, 81

Little Dipper: 24, 48–50

longitude: 15, 34, 69, 76–83, 86, 88, 89, 92, 94

Lull, Ramon: 45

Lyons, Harold: 110

Marrison, Warren A.: 101, 102

Mastrofini, Marco: 10, 14, 119

Mayans: 6, 7

Mechanical clock: 66–69

metric time: 118—120

microwave energy: 110, 111

millennium bug: 119

moon: 3–6

nocturnal: 35, 44–50, 105

North Pole: 10, 21–24, 34, 45, 77, 92, 95

North Star: 24, 33, 44, 45,49, 50

Northern Hemisphere: 10, 13, 32, 45

Nuremburg Egg: 71

oil clock: 52, 59

pendulum clock: 62, 69, 73–76, 85, 99, 105

piezoelectricity: 100–102

planets: 67, 73, 76, 87

Polaris: see North Star

Pope Gregory XIII: 10, 14

prime meridian: 77, 81, 82, 89, 92

protractor: 24–28, 46, 47

Ptolemy: 22

quadrant: 15, 23, 24, 81

quartz: 99–103, 109, 113, 126

radar: 110

radioactivity: 100, 101, 109

radio telescope: 109, 113, 114

railway time: 86, 87

relativity: 117, 121–125

rolling ball clock: 55, 56

Rome, Romans: 6, 8–11, 20, 38, 41, 60

Royal Greenwich Observatory: 86–88, 92, 100, 102

sandglass: see hourglass

satellite: 113–115

Seleucids, Seleucid Dynasty: 17, 20

sextant: 23, 45, 70

shadow clock: 15–21, 35, 51, 99, 105, 126

sidereal day: 83–85

solar day: 83–85, 118

South Pole: 10, 21–23, 34, 77, 92, 95

Southern Hemisphere: 10, 13, 32, 45

Sputnik: 114, 115

stars: 6, 16, 19, 21, 35, 44–50, 73, 84–87, 92, 123, 125, 126

stopwatch: 106, 108

summer solstice: 10, 12

sundial: 15, 20–23, 25–35, 39, 42, 51, 56, 57, 59, 67, 68, 81, 105

Su Sung: 40, 41, 61, 62, 67

telegraph: 86, 87

Thirteenth General Conference on Weights and Measures: 112

time stick: see shadow clock

time zone: 34, 81, 83, 85, 86, 88–98, 117

Tower of Winds: 38–40

Western Hemisphere: 81, 82
winter solstice: 10, 11, 121
World Calendar: 10, 14
Zech, Jacob: 71
Zulu time: 93